The Essex & Suffolk River Stour Navigation

The rebuilt Stour lighter moored at Quay Basin, Sudbury, shortly after reopening in 1980. Both the restoration of the lighter and the reopening of the quay were achieved thanks to Government-sponsored job creation schemes.

THE ESSEX & SUFFOLK RIVER STOUR NAVIGATION

JOHN MARRIAGE

First published 2001

Reprinted in 2014 by
The History Press
The Mill, Brimscombe Port,
Stroud, Gloucestershire, GL5 2QG
www.thehistorypress.co.uk

© The Estate of John Marriage, 2001, 2014

The right of John Marriage to be identified as the Author
of this work has been asserted in accordance with the
Copyrights, Designs and Patents Act 1988.

All rights reserved. No part of this book may be reprinted
or reproduced or utilised in any form or by any electronic,
mechanical or other means, now known or hereafter invented,
including photocopying and recording, or in any information
storage or retrieval system, without the permission in writing
from the Publishers.

British Library Cataloguing in Publication Data.
A catalogue record for this book is available from the British Library.

ISBN 978 0 7524 2350 0

Printed in Great Britain.

All the original locks on the river were crudely built of timber to a very simple design, as depicted in this sketch.

Contents

Introduction		7
1.	Sudbury to Bures	11
2.	Bures to Nayland	45
3.	Nayland to Stratford St Mary	65
4.	Stratford St Mary to Dedham	77
5.	Dedham to Flatford	85
6.	Flatford to Brantham and Mistley	95
7.	Restoring a Lighter	121
The River Stour Trust		127
Acknowledgements		128

IV. ANNE, Cap. XV. An Act for making the river Stower navigable, from the town of Maningtree in the county of Essex, to the town of Sudbury in the county of Suffolk.

A.D. 1705.

WHEREAS the clearing and effecting of a passage for barges, boats, and other vessels by the river Stower, from the town of Maningtree in the county of Essex, to the town of Sudbury in the county of Suffolk, will be very beneficial to trade, advantageous to the poor, and convenient for the conveyance of coals, and other goods and merchandizes, to and from the said towns and parts adjacent, and will very much tend to the employing and encrease of watermen and seamen, and be a means to preserve the highways in and near the said counties and towns; be it therefore enacted by the queen's most excellent majesty, by and with the advice and consent of the lords spiritual and temporal, and commons in this present parliament assembled, and by the authority of the same, that the mayor and aldermen of Sudbury aforesaid for the time being, and Thomas Carter, Roger Scarlin, John Parish, Robert Girling, Henry Crossman, Robert Sparrow, Thomas Hall, Thomas Firmin, Daniel Hasel, and Thomas Robinson, all of Sudbury aforesaid, gentlemen, their heirs and assigns, or such person and persons as they, or any seven or more of them, shall nominate and appoint under their hands and seals, their deputies, agents, officers, workmen and servants, shall be and are hereby authorized and impowered, at their proper costs and charges, to make the said river of Stower navigable, portable and passable for barges, boats, keels, lighters, and other vessels, from the said town of Maningtree to the town of Sudbury, aforesaid ; and from time to time to continue, support, maintain and use such navigation, in such manner as they shall think fit, and for that purpose to clear, scour, open, enlarge or strengthen the said river of Stower, and to dig and cut the banks thereof, and to clear, scour, cut open, or dig the banks of any other stream, brook or beck, that shall to them seem convenient for bringing water into the said river Stower, and thereby making the said river more navigable, portable and passable for boats, barges, lighters, and other vessels ; and to make new and larger cuts, trenches or passages for water, in, upon or through the lands or grounds joining or contiguous to the said river, and to such other streams and brooks as run into the same, as they shall think fit or necessary for the more convenient, easy and better carrying on and effecting the said works and navigation, being the soil or ground of the queen's most excellent majesty, her heirs and successors, or of any other person or persons, bodies politick or corporate, their heirs or successors; and to remove and take away all trees, roots, gravelbeds, or any other impediments whatsoever, which may any ways hinder navigating any boats, barges, lighters, or other vessels, in or upon the said river, either in sailing or hailing thereof, with men, horses, or otherwise, and to build, erect and set up, and make upon any of the lands adjoining to the said river, locks, wears, turnpikes, pens for water, cranes, wharfs and warehouses, where they the said undertakers, their heirs and assigns shall think fit, and to alter, repair and amend the same, as often as they shall think convenient, and to make any ways, passages, and other conveniences, for carrying or conveying of commodities, and other things to and from the said river, with free liberty of ways for carrying and conveying all manner of timber, stone and other materials, for making the said dams, locks, wears and turnpikes, and for repairing the same, from time to time, as there shall be occasion, and to do all other necessary matters and things for the improvement and maintaining of the said navigable passages, streams and premises, or any part thereof, and for amending and heightening any wears or dams, now upon the said river, or amending and altering any bridges whatsoever, or turning or altering any highways in and upon the said river, as may any ways hinder the said passage and navigation ; as also to make, set out, and appoint towing-paths, and ways convenient for towing and drawing of boats, barges and lighters, passing in, through and upon the said river, the said undertakers, their heirs and assigns, first giving satisfaction to the owners and proprietors of the wears, mills, lands, hereditaments and premises respectively, for any damage or injury that shall or may happen to such mills, wears, lands and hereditaments, by making or continuing the said river navigable, as the commissioners hereafter named for that purpose shall direct and appoint ; and such satisfaction shall be likewise given for the said towing-paths, as the said commissioners shall in like manner appoint, in case the said undertakers, their heirs and assigns, shall not before-hand have agreed with the proprietors of such wears, mills, lands and hereditaments respectively, concerning the same.

II. And for the better effecting the premises, and due rating the value of the matters and things to be compounded for, according to the true intent and meaning of this act, if the person concerned, as aforesaid, shall not agree amongst themselves ; be it enacted by the authority aforesaid, that the right honourable the Earl of Dysert of the kingdom of Scotland, the right honourable Henry lord Walden, the right honourable the lord Huntingtower, the honourable Spencer Compton, Esq. the honourable Benjamin Mildmay, Esq. Sir Thomas Hanmere, Sir Francis Masham, Sir Robert Davers, Sir Thomas Felton, Sir Gervase Elwes, Sir Charles Barrington, Sir Dudley Cullum, Sir Robert Barnardiston, Sir Samuel Barnardiston, Sir Thomas Robinson, Sir Robert Kemp, Sir Edmund Bacon, Sir Charles Blois, Sir Henry Dutton Colt, Sir Thomas Webster, Sir Cane James, Sir Simon Dewse, Sir Philip Parker, Baronets ; Sir Isaac Rebow, Sir Thomas Davall, Sir John Marshall, Sir Edward Turner, Sir Joseph Jekyll, Sir Henry Johnson, Sir Joseph Brand, Sir Richard Gipps, Sir Thomas Cook, Knights ; Henry Poley, John Bence, Philip Skippon, Aubry Porter, William Johnson, John Comyns, sergeant at law, Thomas Wild, George Dashwood, Harvey Elwes, John Robinson, John Gourdon, Thomas Williams, George Golding, John Rouse, Robert Honeywood, John Tyndale, Thomas Brand, Thomas Brand, Joseph Brand, John Eldred, sen. John Canham, Samuel Warner, Samuel Gibbs, Bartholomew Young, Samuel Brand, John Eldred, jun. Andrews Warner

The River Stower [sic] Navigation Act of 1705 authorised the Mayor and Aldermen of Sudbury, together with a number of other named persons, to improve the river enabling it to be used by barges, boats, keels, lighters and other vessels. By 1780 nearly all the persons named had died and an amending Act was passed to appoint new commissioners. Both Acts remained on the Statute book until repealed by the Anglian Water Authority Act of 1977 when the navigation rights were transferred to that body. Currently they are administered by the Environment Agency.

Introduction

The River Stour is one of the major rivers of East Anglia. It rises four miles north-west of Haverhill and follows a tortuous course of about fifty miles, passing through many beautiful towns and villages, including Sudbury and Dedham, before it joins the North Sea at Harwich. For much of the way it forms the county boundary between Suffolk and Essex. Its valley is wide, mostly in agricultural use and in part well wooded, with towns and villages of great charm and many historical associations. At Brantham, twenty-three miles below Sudbury, the river becomes tidal.

There is evidence to suggest that some form of traffic was using the freshwater part of the river from early historic times and that this traffic penetrated many miles upstream. However, the first recorded thoughts on making the river suitable for more extensive traffic date from 1628 when King Charles I made grants of Letters Patent to Arnold Spencer to make the river navigable. Already in 1618 he had made part of the River Ouse suitable for barge traffic. It is not clear what success there was on the Stour as in 1705 an Act of Parliament was passed 'for making the river navigable from the town of Manningtree, in the county of Essex, to the town of Sudbury, in the county of Suffolk'. The Act authorised the construction of new channels, locks and other works so as to permit the passage of barges, boats, lighters and other vessels up the twenty-four miles of river between the two towns. In 1780 a further Act was passed to amend the original one and to appoint new commissioners. This was necessary owing to the personal nature of the first Act: all but two of the original commissioners had died, and there was no power under the first Act to appoint replacements.

The navigation works were of an extremely crude nature, although this was to be expected on such an early navigation. Originally, there were thirteen pound locks and thirteen staunches, or flash locks, between Sudbury and Brantham. All were built entirely of timber and the pound locks had a number of crossbeams, or lintels, some six or so feet above the water, intended to prevent the locks from collapsing inwards. This was a feature almost unique to the Stour. As could be expected, the staunches were very unpopular with millers, particularly in dry weather, owing to the vast amount of water they wasted each time a boat passed through and which otherwise would be used to power the mill wheels.

A basin was dug at Sudbury, and wharves and warehouses built. Short cuts and wharves were also built at various points along the course to serve the villages and mills. A particularly long cut of over half a mile in length was constructed at Ballingdon to provide access to chalk pits and brick kilns.

The lighters, as the barges on the river were known, were mostly built at a special basin at Flatford, where major repairs were also carried out. The boats were strikingly similar to those used on the fens

THE ESSEX AND SUFFOLK RIVER STOUR NAVIGATION

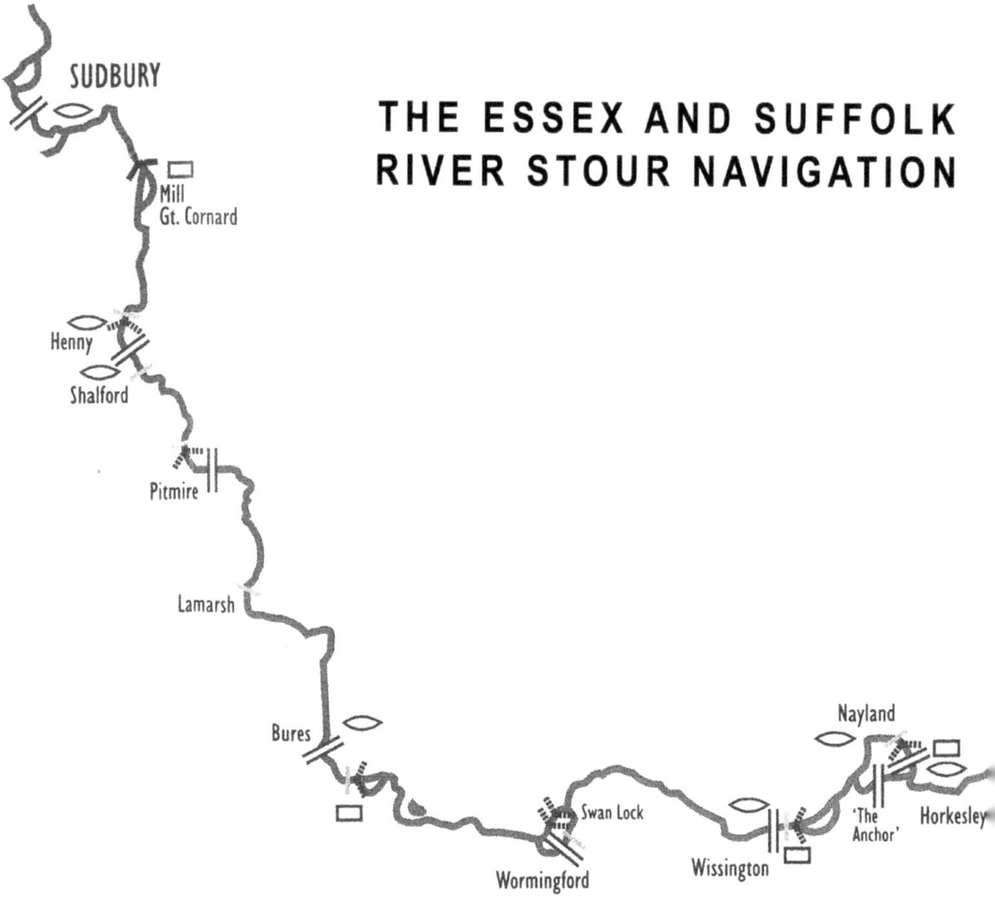

The privately-owned Edwardian steam launch *Firebird* approaching Quay Basin, Sudbury, June 2000.

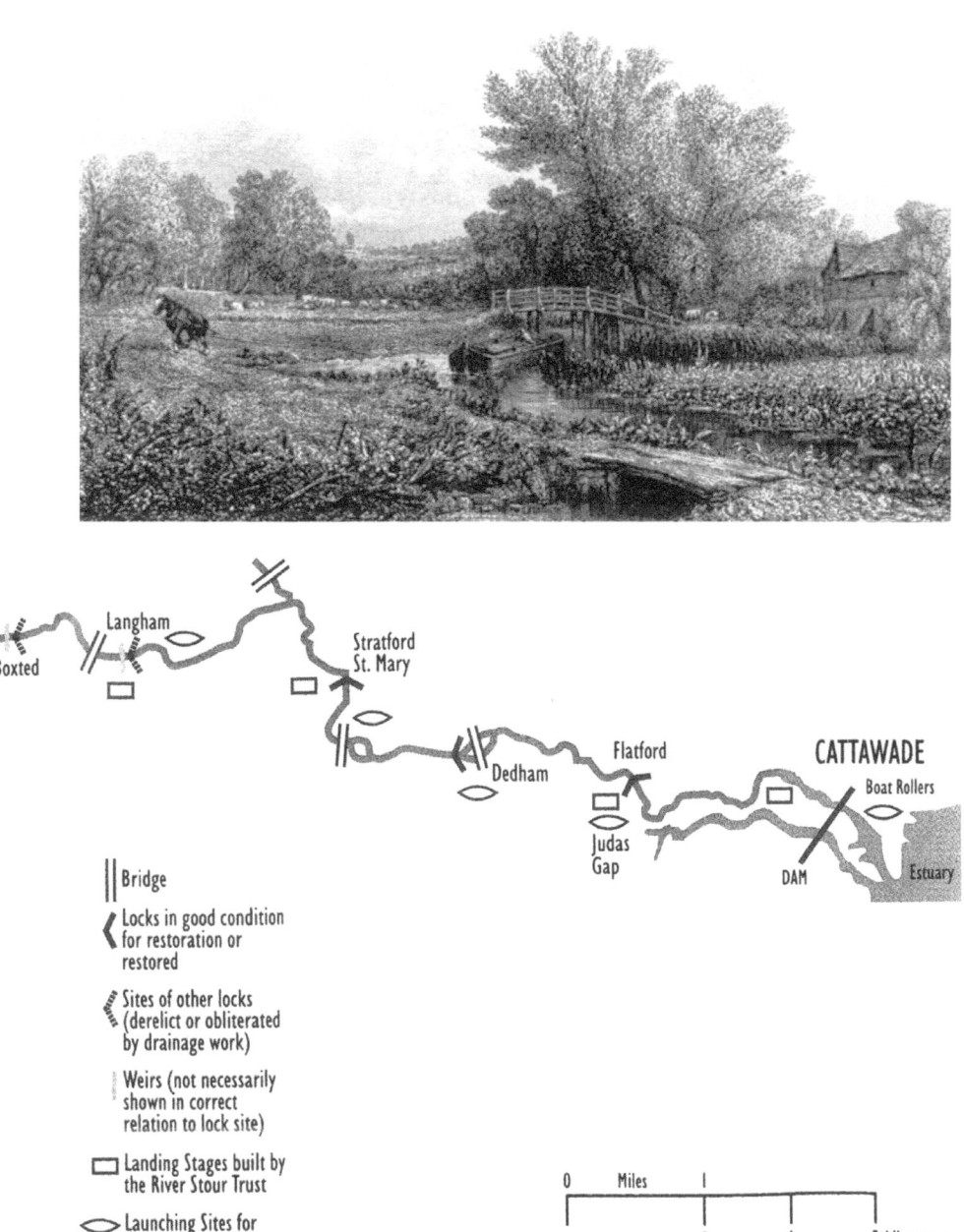

This copy of an engraving shows a gang (pair) of lighters proceeding up river near Great Henny c.1710, probably carrying coal for Sudbury.

and connecting waterways, and used identical terminology. This, together with the likeness of the early-flash locks to those of the Fens, gives rise to the suspicion that Arnold Spencer did actually make some sort of start on improving the river for navigation. Nevertheless, traditional construction methods based on those of coastal barges were preferred to those of the more conventional canal craft. This was to be expected in view of the proximity of Flatford to the estuary, where most of the craftsmen would normally have been working on other types of boat construction.

The lighters usually operated in pairs known as a 'gang' and were drawn by a single horse. The aft boat was called the 'house lighter' and had a cabin for the two-man crew. Each boat was 47ft long by 10ft 9in wide and carried 13 tons of cargo. Both vessels were able to pass through the locks together, shackled stem to stern.

Scenes of the river showing the working craft are a feature of many of the paintings of John Constable, the popular eighteenth century English landscape artist, who lived for a time at Flatford Mill. In order for the cargoes to be transhipped to and from coastal vessels and ships, the lighters were floated on the tide from Brantham, to and from Mistley Quay. Bricks, mostly made at Ballingdon, were the major bulk cargo, and many were shipped to London. Coal was a substantial return cargo.

The coming of the railways in the mid-nineteenth century started a long decline in the use of canals and river navigations throughout the country and the Stour was no exception. At first, there was keen competition between the rival modes of transport. To improve navigation, six new pound locks were built to replace the old staunch locks. In addition, tolls were reduced and experiments conducted into the use of a steam-powered barge. However none of these measures helped and by the outbreak of the First World War there remained little through-traffic. On the upper section, a number of lighters were carrying on the traditional traffic of transporting bricks from the kilns at Ballingdon, but only to Sudbury railway station, where they completed their journey by rail. Finally, as a wartime measure, the Admiralty ordered that the remaining lighters be sunk at Ballingdon to ensure they did not fall into enemy hands if the country was invaded. The unfortunate horses were shot. However, on the lower section, a pair of boats con-tinued to trade from Mistley to Dedham until 1928 by carrying grain to the mill.

Following the loss of trade and money the navigation works quickly deteriorated and were soon unusable. However, in the early 1930s four locks on the lower section of the river, at Stratford St Mary, Dedham, Flatford and Brantham, were rebuilt by the then South Essex Waterworks Company, in return for the navigation company agreeing not to oppose proposals to abstract water from the river. These new locks were built to the same dimensions as the originals but with concrete chambers. As a concession to the old design at Flatford, lintels and facsimile timber-work, although not physically necessary, were included in the new structure. Sadly, before the new works were complete, the navigation company was dissolved for financial reasons. Use of the new locks was confined to occasional pleasure craft, though a boat builder at Dedham delivered new craft to estuary customers via Flatford and Brantham. However, no organisation remained either to maintain the navigation or collect any tolls, and the new locks slowly became unusable.

Concurrently with the passing of the Anglian Water Authority Act on 19th March 1977, the original navigation acts were repealed. They were replaced by the new Act, the most important provision being that the Water Authority (now the Environment Agency) also became the navigation authority. By then the old timber locks above Stratford St Mary had totally disappeared or were in a ruinous state, even though light craft were continuing to use the entire river for recreation.

In 1968, the River Stour Trust Ltd, a registered charity allied to the Inland Waterways Association, was formed. It has since followed an active programme of restoration, excavating most of the old terminal Basin at Sudbury, restoring to use two of the three concrete locks and building an entirely new lock at Cornard. It also operates two Edwardian-style electric launches and has its headquarters in a Grade II listed building. Its ambition is to continue its restoration works along the river, with the object of re-opening the full twenty-four mile navigation for a more extended range of pleasure boating. These projects are receiving increasing public support.

One
Sudbury to Bures

Quay Basin, and its arm Gasworks Cut, created soon after the passing of the first Stour Navigation Act, were the main terminals at Sudbury, where two large buildings were erected for the storage of goods and material brought up the river. Here, c.1900, the occupants of a rowing boat explore the water area.

Following the decline in barge traffic, Quay Basin, Gasworks Cut and the adjoining granaries became derelict. This shows the basin c.1950, when it presented an unsightly appearance, with little water remaining.

In the late 1970s, the River Stour Trust, with the aid of a government-sponsored job creation scheme, restored part of the old basin. At the same time a separate group acquired the derelict granary and converted it into an amateur theatre. When this picture was taken work had just started on the construction of new concrete wharf edging around the perimeter of the basin.

In a year-long project the Trust used ten previously unemployed men to remove the accumulated rubble and silt from the basin and to build new retaining walls. Here, despite the filthy working conditions, this young man manages to remain cheerful!

Two of his colleagues pause in their efforts to dig a trench to accommodate the new retaining wall.

A view of the newly re-opened Quay Basin with the Trust's restored lighter moored alongside in 1980. An important part of the undertaking was the construction of a completely new wharf alongside the recently opened Quay Theatre. This was necessary to operate the theatre, as well as provide mooring space. The facing bricks – known as Ballingdon Reds – were made at a brickyard some 200yds away and reclaimed from a demolished warehouse at Mistley.

The same scene, June 2000. The restored Basin is now a Mecca for boat enthusiasts. Oarsmen from the adjacent premises of the long established Sudbury Rowing Club are very frequent users.

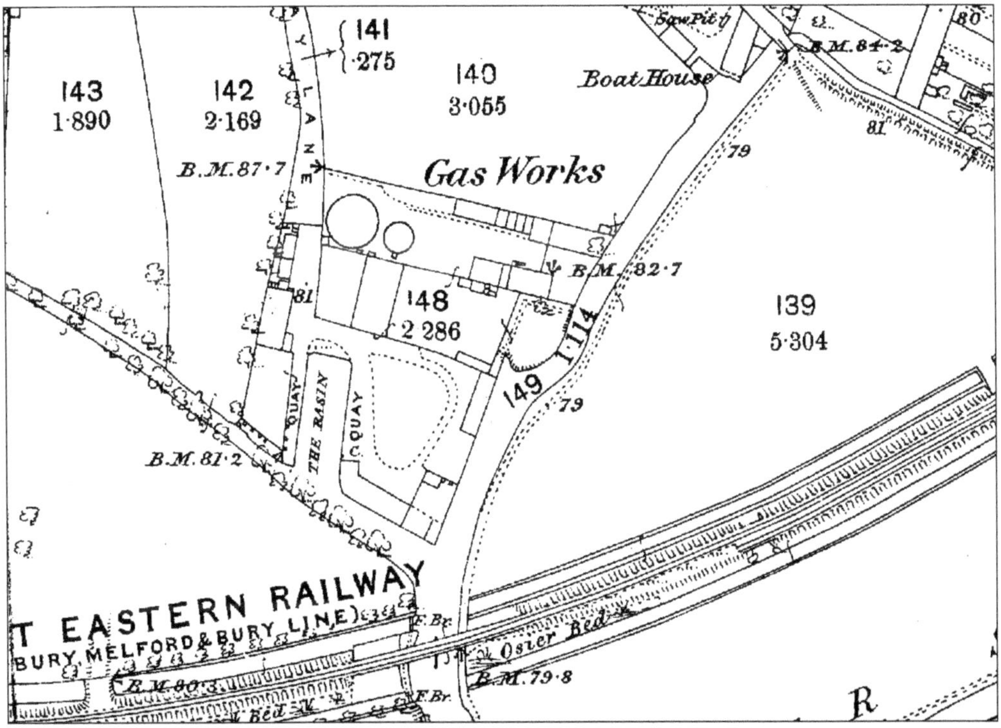

This extract from a nineteenth century Ordnance Survey map shows the main terminus of the Stour Navigation at Sudbury. There were quays on both sides of the main basin and a direct access to the town centre by Quay Lane. A second arm of the basin, known as Gasworks Cut, penetrated a further 100yds towards the town centre, to terminate at a winding hole. It is reputed that some Stour lighters were built next to this turning place. Two substantial brick warehouses were quickly built alongside the two artificial channels. The larger is now an amateur theatre, whilst the other – with access to Gasworks Cut – is the headquarters of the River Stour Trust.

Lord Greenwood of Rossendale, first President of the River Stour Trust, declares the restored Quay Basin open for use in September 1980.

The 819th Civil Engineering Squadron of the United States Air force restored Gasworks Cut as a training exercise in 1985. It was then completely overgrown, with the adjacent granary long since empty and derelict. This was the scene in 1975.

After the USAF completed the restoration of Gasworks Cut, the River Stour Trust stationed their newly restored lighter (see chapter 8, page 121) alongside the still disused granary, which they only officially took over some years later.

Gasworks Cut and The Granary, May 2000.

The boat slip into Gasworks Cut is the only launching facility for trailed boats at present existing along the navigation apart from a set of boat rollers at Brantham at the other end of the waterway.

Anthony Marriage steers *Araminta*, owned by Robin Jones, along the Sudbury reach, July 2000. In summer, the river attracts people of all ages.

The old towpath alongside Gasworks Cut lives on as a public footpath albeit under the name of 'Mayor's Walk'. However, its original character still survives where it passes under the old railway bridge.

As an artificial channel, the entrance to the Quay Basin complex from the main river channel requires regular dredging, which is carried out with land based machinery.

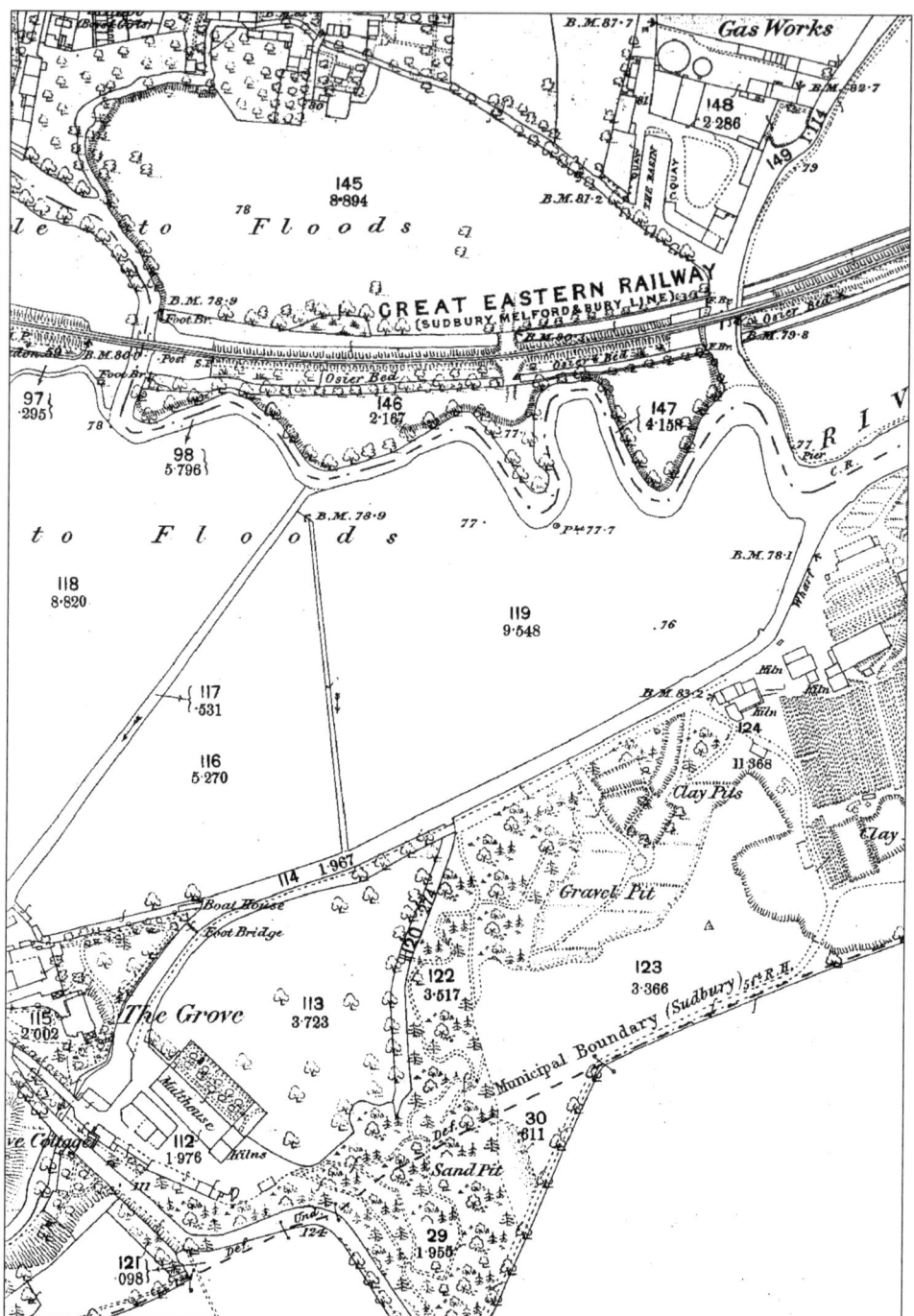

Most of the half-mile long cut, which leads from the river towards Ballingdon, is shown on this turn of the twentieth century Ordnance Survey map. In Victorian times, a cluster of important activities took place at the head of the channel, including digging out chalk and clay and the manufacture of huge quantities of bricks. The latter were exported by barge to many parts of East Anglia and beyond. In 2000, the silted cut was re-dredged as a drainage channel. However, the last section of the cut, which tunnelled under Middleton Road, remains infilled.

Ballingdon Cut fell into disuse at the time of the First World War, when some fourteen lighters were deliberately sunk bow to stern inland from the entrance of the cut to the river. This 1960s picture shows the skeleton of one protruding from the enveloping mud and reeds.

In the early 1970s the newly formed River Stour Trust set about digging out the remains of one of the old vessels. Although the upper works had rotted away, remarkably it was found that the hull still floated. It was later towed away for eventual restoration.

In the 1980s, as the result of renovations to a property at the head of Ballingdon Cut, the remains of the only steam driven barge ever to have operated on the navigation were discovered. Unfortunately, although the massive prop-shaft and propeller remained, the actual engine had obviously been removed.

The remains of the steam lighter were subsequently given to the Trust and removed by lorry to Dedham, where they are now on display.

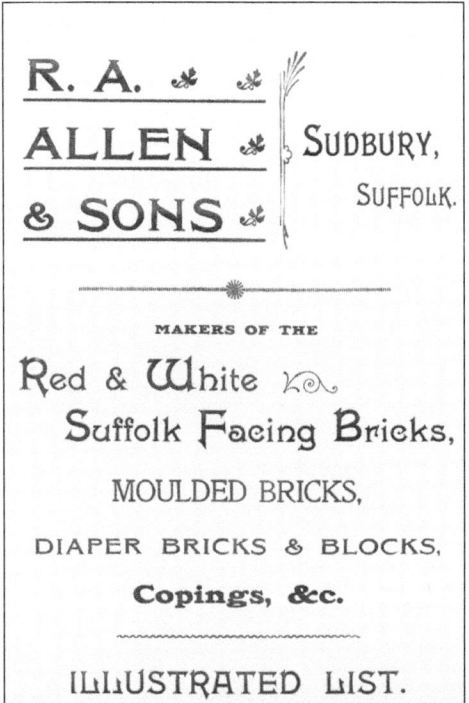

The firm of R.A. Allen were the owners of a substantial industrial complex at the head of Ballingdon Cut. Extracts of their brochure, c.1900, reproduced here, give details of red and grey moulded clay bricks made at the works. The company was also a substantial shareholder in the Navigation Company and for this reason the steam barge was moored at their private wharf.

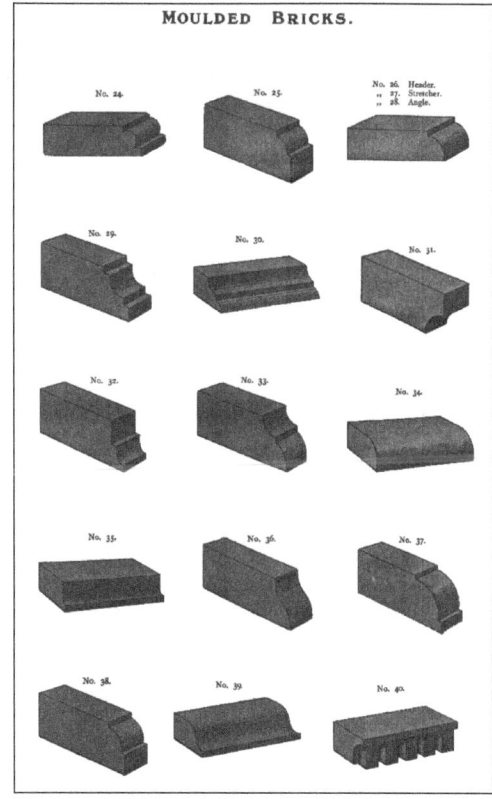

The restored lighter *John Constable* being towed along the river at Friars Meadow, Sudbury by *Snowy*, led by Mrs Francis Batten, *c.*1980.

In Victorian times the Stour Boat Club (now Sudbury Rowing Club) was established at a wharf at Quay Basin and rowing became a significant part of the town's social life. Here, c.1930, a coxed four were captured on film leaving their quay. The Club still provides an important sports facility in the town and is one of only two clubs in Suffolk. The crew were (left to right): Brian Bacon (cox), Ted Eady, Frank Maynard and Jimmy Osborne.

In the late 1950s the local committee of the Inland Waterways Association started holding annual canoe races downstream from Friars Meadow, Sudbury to Bures and Nayland. Today, the Braintree Canoe Club holds races over a similar course.

This copy of a early eighteenth century engraving depicts a pair of lighters approaching Cornard Lock. In the distance is Great Cornard Parish Church. In common with the other original locks on the river, the chamber was made entirely of timber, with stout crossbeams preventing the walls bowing inwards.

Although Cornard lock has been rebuilt several times, it became derelict in the 1920s. In postwar years an automatic weir was built on its site. In 1999, the River Stour Trust built an entirely new lock alongside. Cornard Mills is seen in the upper picture.

Cornard Mills, *c.*1900, was one of the larger water mills on the Stour and made extensive use of the river for transporting wheat and flour. Until 1880 it had a weather-boarded exterior but was then brick faced with locally made 'Suffolk Whites'. It has since been greatly extended and now produces pet food.

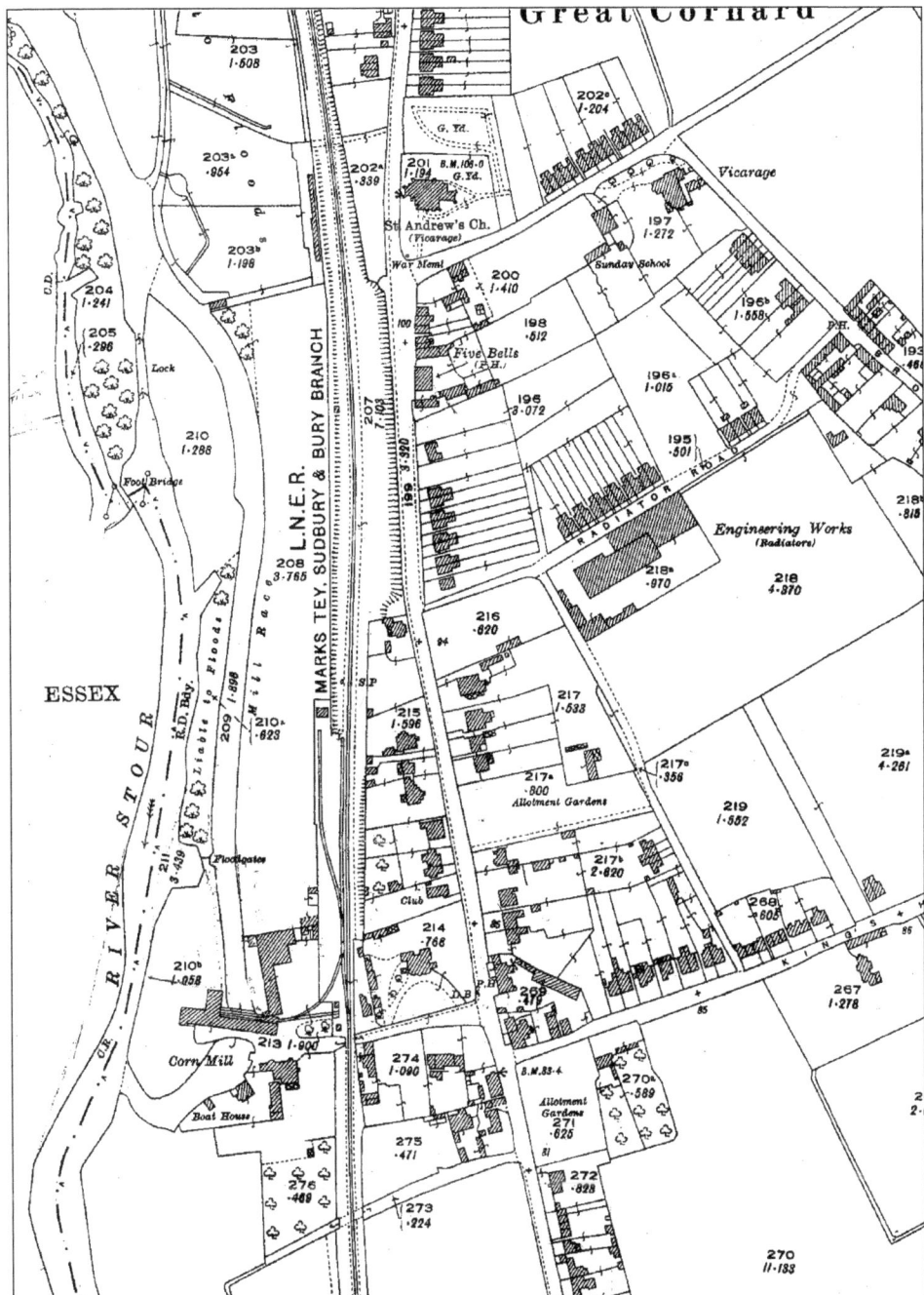

This pre-1938 map shows Cornard Mills with its long mill race. The original 1905 lock is thought to have been built midway along the mill-island, on the site of the small indentation indicated in the bank. Later, when the navigation was improved, it was replaced as shown on the plan. In the 1950s an automatic weir was built on the site. In 1999, the River Stour Trust, with the aid of a grant from the Millennium Commission, constructed a new lock almost exactly on the site of the 1705 lock.

The river has always been used for recreation and many riparian owners had boats. Here, a mother and son wait for father (probably the photographer) to open Cornard Lock, c.1900.

Horse-drawn barges were used regularly to take parties on short trips. The hatch covers were useful vantage-points for deck chairs, from where the slowly unfolding scenery could be watched.

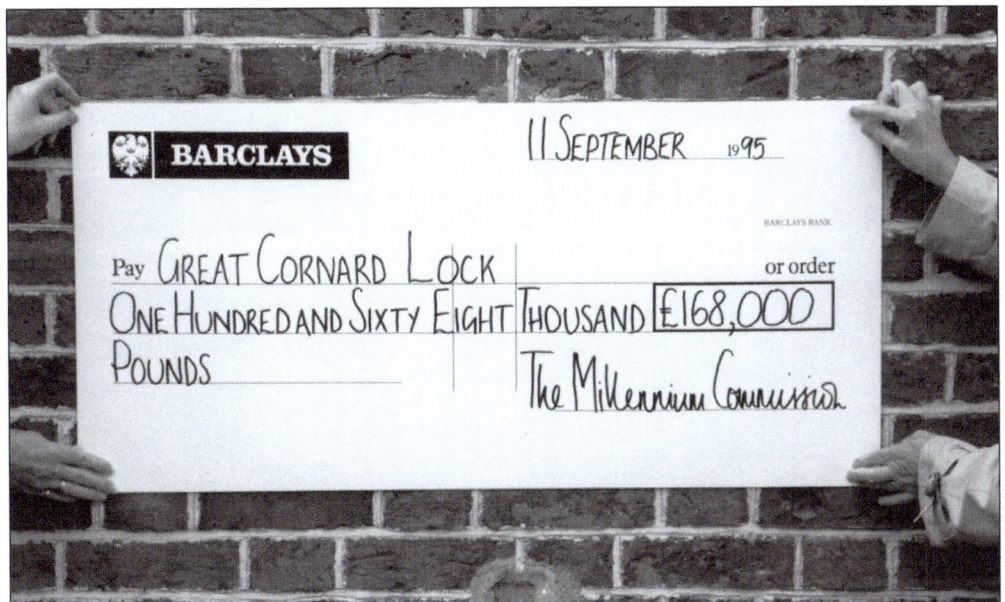

In 1995, after considerable negotiations, the River Stour Trust announced that the Millennium Commission had awarded the Trust a grant towards the construction of an entirely new lock at Great Cornard. This was one of a handful of Millennium projects approved in East Anglia. Few of these were awarded to voluntary groups.

The contract to build a new lock, 15.25m long by 3.75m wide, was awarded to May Gurney of Norwich, and was started early in 1997. Unlike the original lock, the chamber was of concrete, with a brick outer skin and steel gates. Although not structurally necessary, crossbeams were included to maintain the traditional appearance. The new lock is considerably shorter than the original, but large enough to accommodate a single Stour lighter.

The new lock was declared open in September 1997. One of the first boats to pass through was the trailed boat *Schandelle*, visiting the waterway especially for the event.

Cornard Lock, from downstream – Open Day, 1997. A variety of craft depart the lock, into Henny reach, led by *Petunia*.

Cornard Lock, viewed from upstream, with boats passing into Sudbury reach, on Open Day, 1997.

Traditionally, members of the Sudbury Club used to row down to the Henny Swan pub at the start of the boating season. Sadly, this custom was discontinued about twenty years ago. Here, pictured around 1980, a coxed four proceeds downstream as part of a rally of boats supporting the developing campaign to restore Cornard Lock.

One of the first steam launches to navigate the Henny Reach after the opening of Cornard Lock in 1997.

Most craft on the river are canoes, skiffs or powered craft. However, a few sailing boats can sometimes be seen gracefully tacking along the river, even though the comparatively narrow channel and overhanging vegetation can cause problems. This dinghy was captured on film c.1990.

Once there were many large mills along the river, each with a lock nearby. Henny Mill was a long, two-storey timber-framed structure, latterly roofed with corrugated iron. It was demolished about 1935. In this picture the navigation channel is masked by the belt of trees on the right.

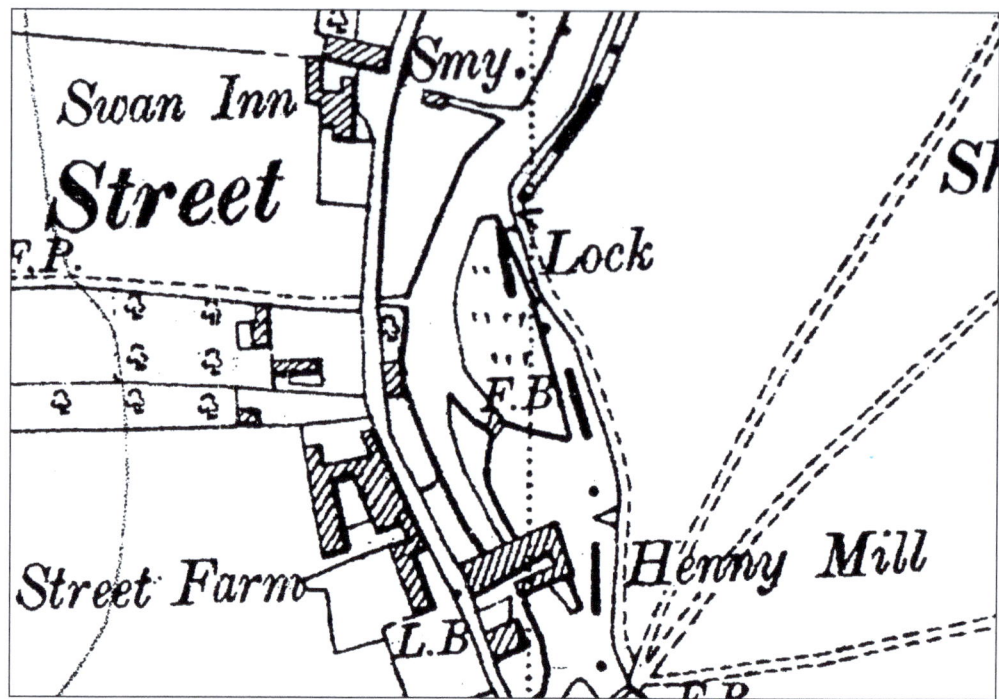

From Victorian times Henny Street has been a popular stop for locals and visitors, with the Henny Swan pub well frequented. Once an attractive Victorian boathouse graced the open riverside frontage but, sadly, this has now gone. More recently, during the summer, the pub has become the terminus for a regular public boat trip from Sudbury.

A Victorian family group in 'Sunday best' happily pose for this picture beside the footpath bridge just below Henny Mill and the mill house. The wooden bridge has since been replaced by a modern structure.

Henny Lock disappeared in the early 1920s and no photograph is known to exist. A simple weir, seen here in June 2000, was later built on the same site to maintain the navigation level. Light craft frequently portage alongside.

Henny floodgates, like most of the installations on the river, was a simple wooden structure, with winding gear fitted to the paddles similar to those on the locks. The footbridge, as well as providing a platform from which to operate the paddles, gave the lock keeper access to the lock. The navigation channel is in the foreground.

At Shalford, midway between Henny and Pitmere, a shallow weir has been built by the Environment Agency to maintain a slight change of water level. To assist in the portaging of small boats, landing stages have been installed above and below.

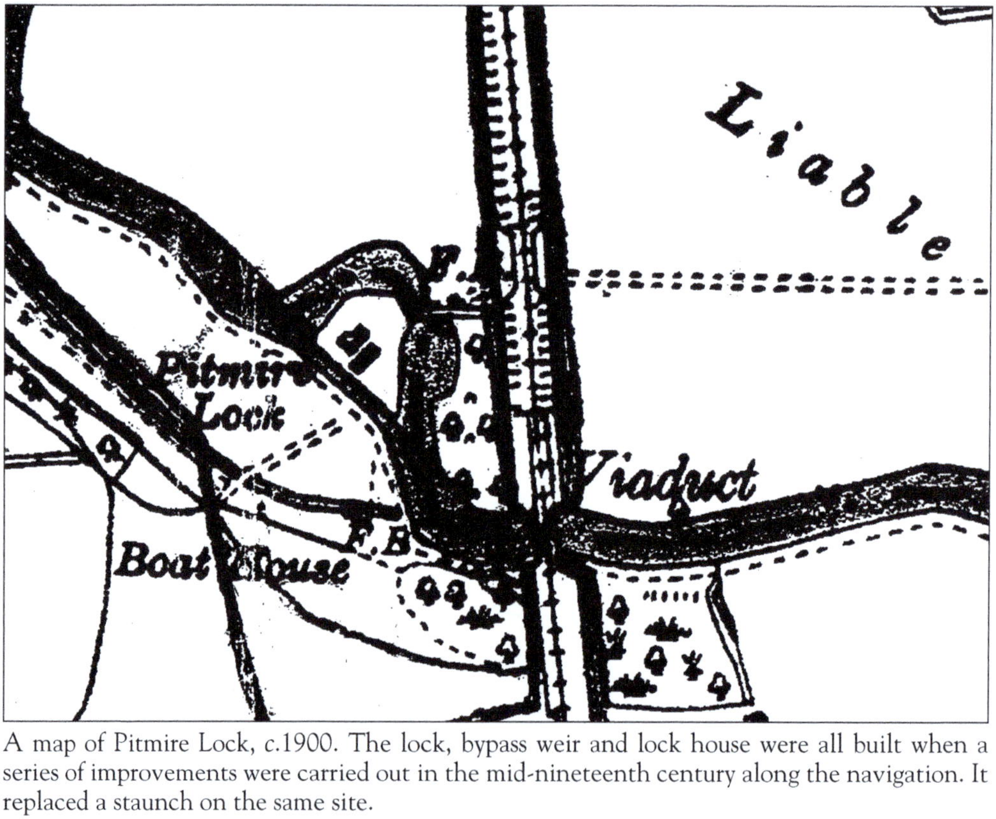

A map of Pitmire Lock, c.1900. The lock, bypass weir and lock house were all built when a series of improvements were carried out in the mid-nineteenth century along the navigation. It replaced a staunch on the same site.

Pitmire Lock, c.1900. The upright timbers and lintels of the lock chamber can be glimpsed in front of the double fronted lock house. The bypass channel was to the rear of the house, where the overflow sluices were sited.

Pitmire lock from downstream. Access to the lock house was by way of the small wooden bridge.

Pitmire Lock in 1926, some years after barge traffic had ceased. Although the lock was still apparently in a reasonable condition, both gates had been pinned open and the head of water on the upper reach lost.

The bypass weir at Pitmire Lock in 1926 when still apparently in working order. The structure is typical of those once found on the Stour. Today, little remains, though the channel still holds water.

In Victorian times craft could be hired from the lock keeper at Pitmire, who had a large boathouse on the Essex bank. Today, this same area is part of a Nature Reserve and still attracts many visitors.

Ernie Broyd was the last lock keeper at Pitmire. He was also navigation foreman, responsible for the upkeep of all the locks, a job he took over from his father who worked for the navigation all his life. Mr Broyd left the river in 1912, when regular barge traffic ceased, and the lock cottage subsequently became vacant. An earlier lock keeper was William Blois, who, in addition to operating the lock, was also responsible for looking after and skippering the steam driven barge with which the Navigation Company experimented throughout the 1860s.

Throughout the 1920s the Nicolson family, of Halstead, rented Pitmere Lock island and the derelict house for weekend and summer use. Extra living space was provided by a large ex-army bell tent. Mr Nicholson was gassed during the Great War and this open-air lifestyle was ideal for his recuperation. He worked locally as surveyor to Halstead Urban District Council.

In the 1920s the derelict lock, with its wooden floor, provided a safe swimming pool.

By the mid 1950s little remained of the lock except for a pair of crossbeams, a few side timbers and, preserved under the water, the floor of the chamber. The house was in process of being demolished, the bricks being carted away.

Today, very little remains of the lock chamber, except for a single crossbeam and a few stakes protruding out of the water, although much of the wooden floor of the chamber still survives. The site is now part of the Daws Hall Nature Reserve, which encompasses the immediate locality.

Two

Bures to Nayland

Bures Mill, pictured here in 1956, is one of the larger former water mills on the river. During the latter years of its working life it acquired a number of unattractive outbuildings and its traditional weather board covering was replaced by ugly asbestos sheeting. Happily, in the last few years the new owner has started a major restoration project thereby recreating its original splendid appearance. In 2000, the owner was presented with a Conservation Award for his restoration work. In the foreground is the author in a canoe.

Bures bridge and the village wharf, *c*.1900, when the busy village made considerable use of the river for transport. Sadly, barge traffic was already declining, having transferred to the nearby railway, built in 1849.

The Boat House at Bures, on the Essex bank of the river, *c*.1900, was a well known rendezvous on Sunday afternoons. Boats were on hire and you could partake of tea and cakes, whilst watching the world go by. Alas, the property is now in private hands and no boat hire is available in the village.

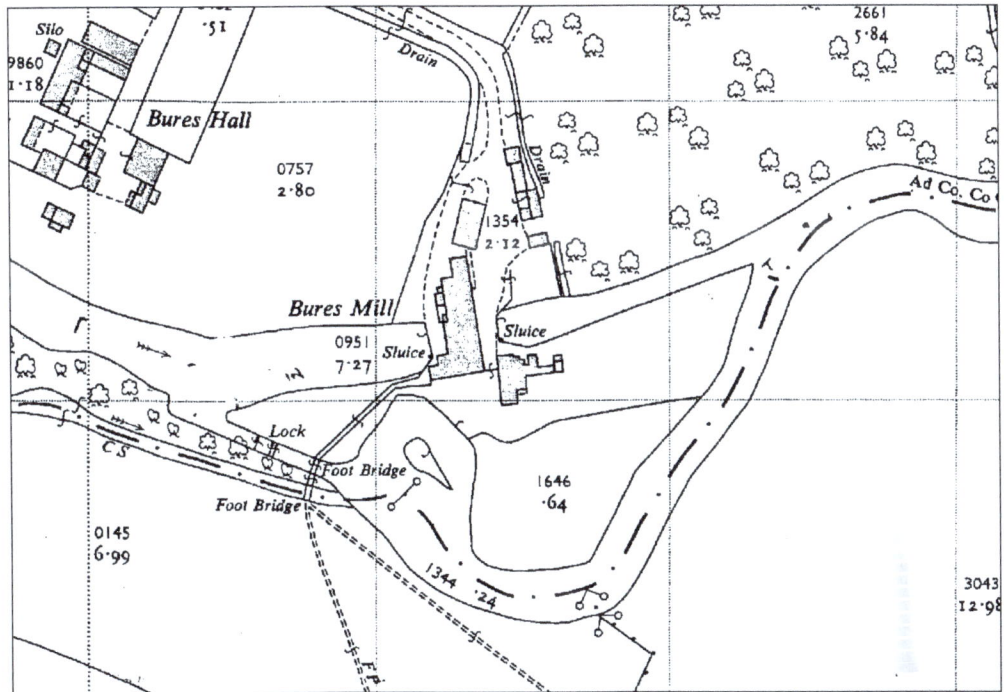

This section of map shows Bures Mill and the adjacent lock as depicted by a cartographer in the 1920s. In 1938, a major flood prevention scheme was carried out on the Bures Reach, with an automatic weir on the lock site, which lowered the water level upstream by about 2ft. Despite this, recent studies have discovered that the depth of water is more than adequate to allow this part of the river to be used by larger recreational craft.

This shot, taken in spring 2000, shows the automatic weir at Bures, coincidentally built a similar size to the original lock. Its design gives rise to speculation that it could be converted to joint navigation/flood control purposes without too much difficulty. The accepted portage route is on the south side

This scene at Bures bridge taken in September 2000 provides a contrast with the upper picture on page 46. The lowering of the water level in 1938 has increased the headroom under the bridge. However, the former wharf area has completely disappeared under a blanket of foliage creating a softer, more rural appearance.

Opposite: A slice of navigation history is enshrined in this 1930s map of Wormingford as it shows both the original 1705 navigation channel through the millpond and the replacement by-pass channel, built in 1838. The newer channel, with two shallow locks, was built to overcome persistent shoaling below the original lock, impossible to remove with the primitive dredgers of the times. The new channel was an improvement recommended to the Navigation company by Mr Cubitt when he visited the waterway in the early nineteenth century. Once barge traffic to Sudbury ceased in the 1920s the newer channel became overgrown and the locks derelict. Today, only a few traces of the two locks survive but the channel still holds water in places. Canoes and other boats using the river now portage around the original lock, since converted into a fixed sluice, passing directly into the millpond, so reverting to the 1705 route.

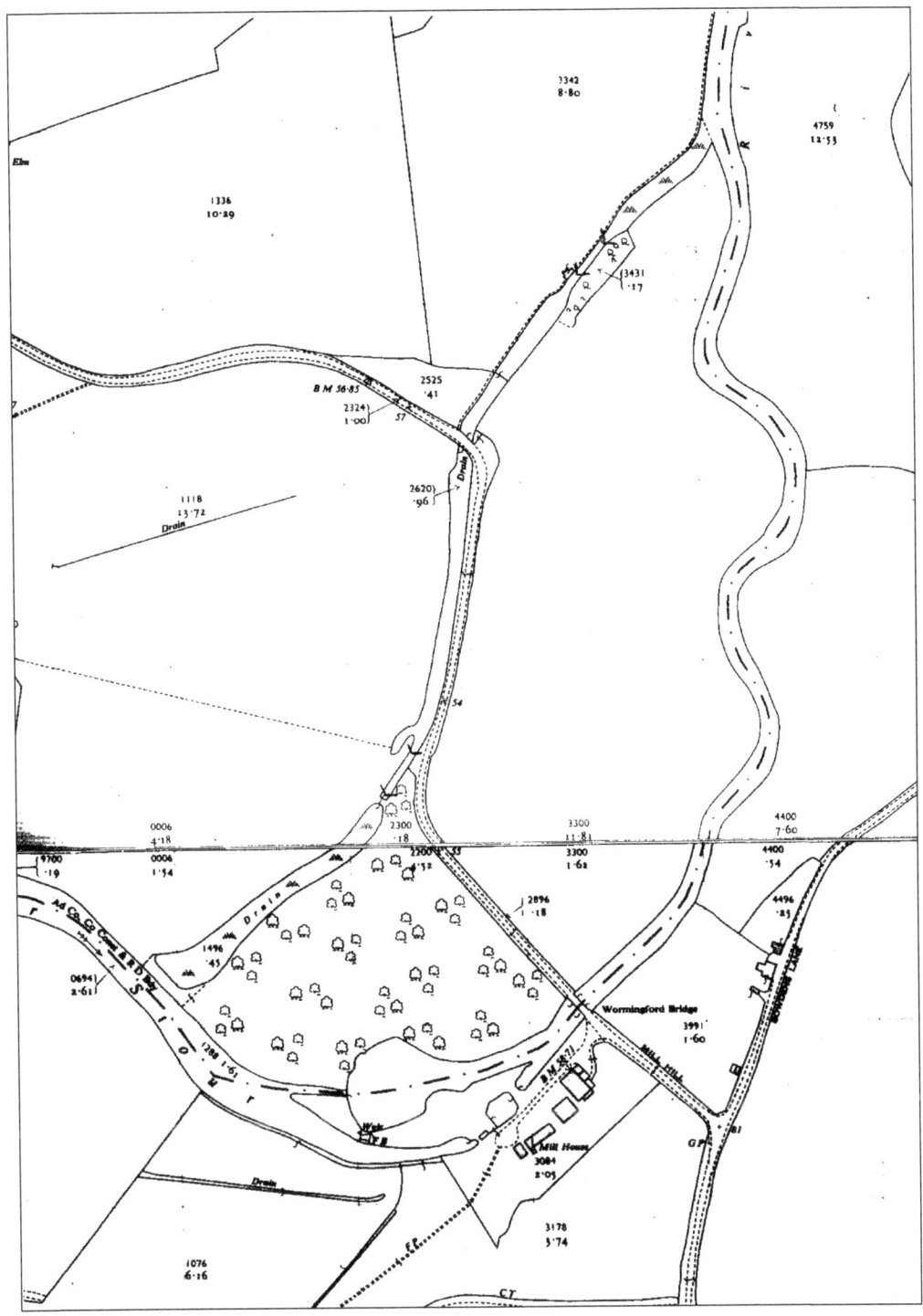

Although now used as a sluice, the original lock can still be identified. The winding mechanism follows that of other bypass weirs along the navigation whilst the outline of the chamber is still marked by a line of stakes.

The original channel leading from the 1705 lock can be seen on the right of this c.1900 picture. It is evident that some of the shoaling problems were caused by a ford crossing the channel from Wormingford Mill.

A pair of lighters – known as a gang – approach Wormingford Lock, c.1900. 200yds further on is Swan Lock.

Lighters passing along Wormingford Cut, c.1900. The channel is now almost dry but remarkably the two large oak trees still survive.

Passing through Wormingford Lock, c.1900. Dredging seems to have taken place recently and the spoil has been levelled.

Swan Lock, Wormingford Cut, c.1900, was a crude structure built of stout timbers driven vertically into the ground and reinforced by upright and horizontal baulks of timber. At either end of the chamber, preventing the entrance and exit from bowing inwards, were three substantial parallel lintels or crossbeams. The gates were opened by pulling a chain fitted to the outside edge. Gate paddles were raised by winding a connecting chain around a horizontal capstan.

A gang of lighters leaving Swan Lock, c.1900. The pair of boats were permanently shackled, bow to stern, with the rear vessel acting as a rudder to the front boat. A long tiller extended from the bow

of the stern vessel to the centre of the lead boat, where there was a small bridge between two holds. This accommodated the steersman. A second member of the two-man crew led the horse.

The ruins of Wormingford Lock, in 1955, when the crossbeams and chamber were collapsing and the channel banked off to prevent an uncontrolled flow of water through the cut. When visited in 2000 only a few broken timbers survived.

The remains of Swan Lock, c.1955. A rickety crossbeam was still in position and the channel held some water. Little change has occurred since then.

Wissington Lock was sited hard against the mill, making a connection from the mill race into the millpond, as seen on this c.1900 map. After barge traffic ceased, the lock gradually became unusable. In 1953, a large horseshoe shaped weir was built in the same place. Present river users portage on the southern bank.

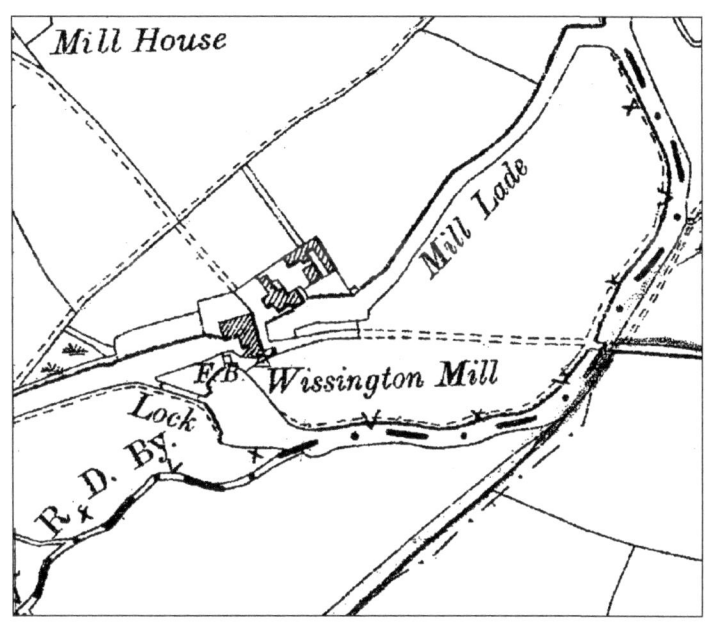

Wissington Mill (also known as Wiston Mill) was – and still is – a large attractive weather boarded structure from where barges took most of the flour down to Mistley. Sadly, it is no longer actively used for milling. The lock crossbeams can be seen in the foreground.

Three pairs of lighters moored in the mill pool, 1894. The plumes of smoke rising from two of the stern boats came from small stoves in the rear cabins and were the crew's only source of hot food and comfort.

Wissington Mill, *c*.1960, framed by its wealth of enveloping trees, provides an attractive view from the millpond.

Maintenance work on the navigation was a round the year occupation – and at times a major problem. Here, navvies are pile-driving stout oak timber along the edge of Wissington millpond, to create a strong retaining wall against erosion.

In 1894, a photographer was on hand to take this picture of Major General Warsley, together with his wife and daughter, enjoying a cruise near Wissington.

When the navigation was in operation, water levels were kept high, as this picture of Wissington Lock shows, c.1890. After barge traffic ceased water levels fell, but since 1953 they have been maintained at a constant level by the weir, built by the water authority.

Working barges – after a good clean out – were often loaned to local groups for leisurely outings. In 1891, over sixty members of the Nayland Chapel, dressed in their Sunday finery, cruised up to Wissington, in a 'gang' of lighters . Days on the river were much enjoyed well before the advent of cheap road and rail trips.

In creating the navigation the proprietors found it necessary to build various bridges along the waterway to replace fords linking the mills and villages. Like the other navigation structures the bridges were of timber and followed a common pattern throughout the entire length of the waterway. This bridge at Wissington allowed cart traffic to cross the river from Suffolk to Essex.

The river viewed from Wissington Mill, May 1894. On the left is the lock, with three clearly visible crossbeams. Waiting to pass through are two 'gangs' of lighters, probably on their way downstream with a cargo from Allen's brickyard at Ballingdon.

Three
Nayland to Stratford St Mary

At the turn of the nineteenth century there were extensive wharves at Nayland, particularly along the mill stream. The mill proprietor, Mr. Stannard, operated a large fleet of barges. On the left of the picture is Nayland Lock house. Although the lock has now disappeared and been replaced by a weir, the house is one of only two surviving lock cottages.

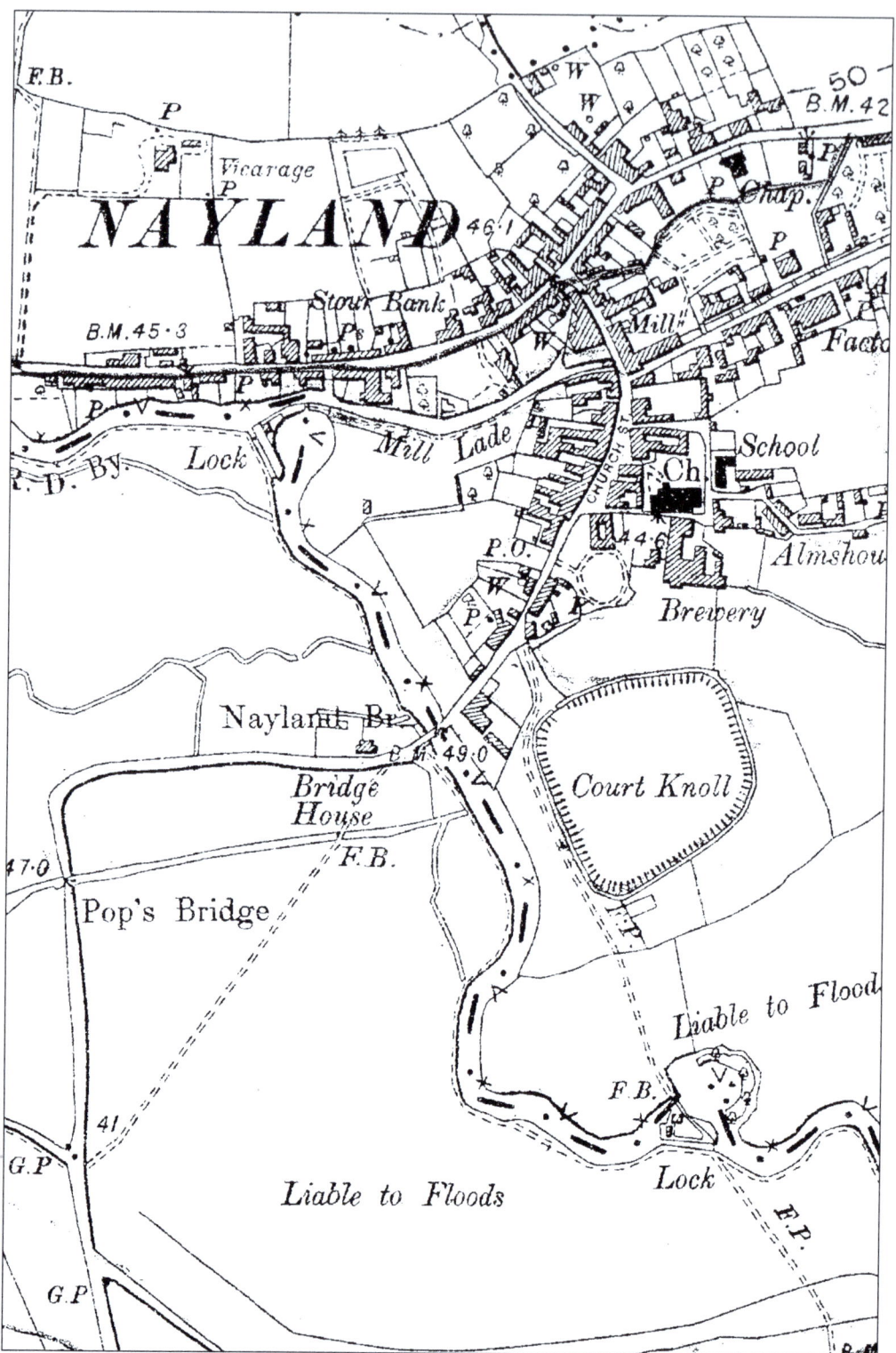

Nayland Lock, c.1900, from downstream Behind are glimpsed several wharf buildings and in the distance, on rising land, the Vicarage provides the incumbent with an excellent view of the river.

Opposite: Nayland Village, as shown on this turn of the twentieth century map. To the west was Nayland Lock, whilst to the south was Horkesley Lock, the halfway point in the navigation. Facilities were provided at the latter for an overnight stop in the form of a 'bothy' or crews bunkhouse. Sadly, since the 1920s, the lock house, bothy, lock and weir have all disappeared, with the result that water levels have fallen between the two lock sites, creating real problems for present day river users. In the 1960s the village was bypassed by a new road leading due north from Pops Bridge, crossing the Stour west of the former lock site, and rejoining the original road.

Unfortunately, the Nayland bypass over the Stour was built with very restricted headroom and width. It presents the most formidable obstruction to long term restoration of full navigation and an alternative route would need to be found.

Another view of Nayland Bypass bridge, June 2000. The current through this narrow channel is often swift, and at the request of boat users, safety chains have been fitted along both walls.

In 1951 Nayland Weir was built on the site of the old lock to a similar design as Wissington. This paddler, seen just below the weir, c.1960, has just portaged his craft.

Nayland Bridge, seen here c.1960, was built to navigation height. It has since been replaced by a new bridge of similar appearance and the 'Bell' keystone has been incorporated within the new arch.

Nayland Wharf, c.1900, with the Anchor pub and the bridge. At the time it was a busy quay, with barges bringing chalk from Ballingdon to local farmers.

Horkesley Lock, c.1900, seen on the left together with the lock house. To the right was the bothy and the bypass weir beyond. Little remains of these, although the sheet of water on the right, known as Horkesley Pool, was restored recently for wildlife conservation.

Another view of Horkesley Lock and Pool, c.1900. In the distance are the Anchor pub and Nayland bridge, emphasising the fact that the two locks were only half a mile apart – almost the shortest pound on the navigation.

A pair of lighters at Great Horkesley, c.1900. Normally, the work-horse was led but sometimes a youth would ride along the towpath. In the centre, the steersman holds the tiller, permanently fitted to the stern vessel.

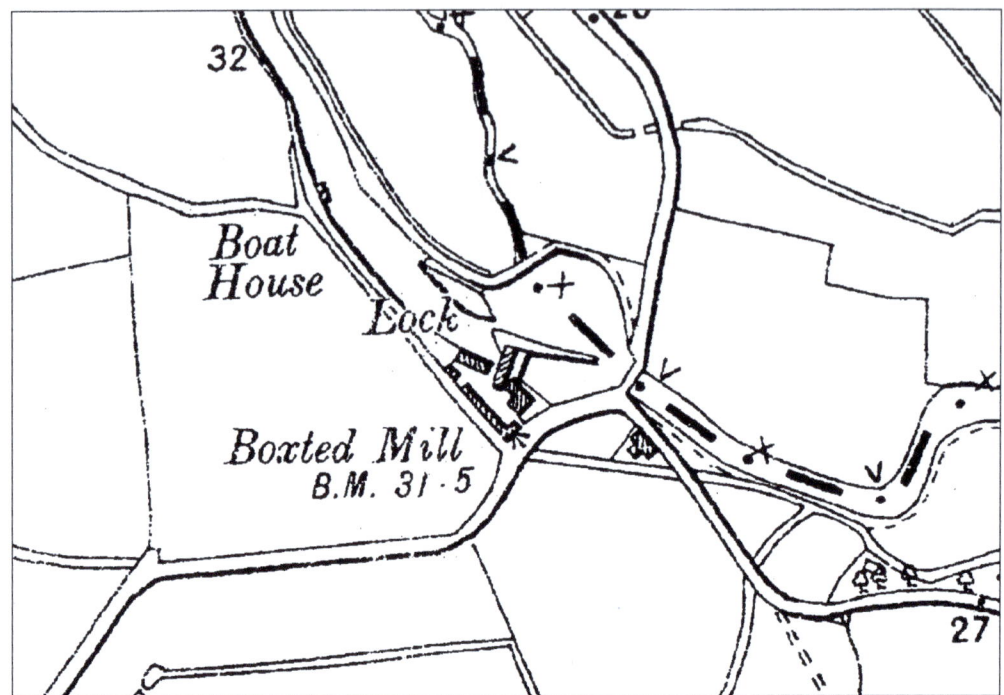

As shown on this c.1900 map, Boxted Mill was downstream from Great Horkesley. The lock was close to the mill, giving direct boat access from the race into the millpond. The house is now a private residence, with the lock site incorporated into the garden. A portage route is nearby.

Since barge traffic ceased, in places the main channel has become shallow and overgrown. This is mainly due to lack of dredging, as on this 1974 picture taken below Boxted bridge. The Mill House is partially obscured by the coach – its passengers probably on one of the popular 'mystery' tours.

Langham Mill was demolished many years ago and few illustrations survive apart from this black and white sketch. A water abstraction station was built on its site in the 1930s and a weir has now replaced the associated lock. The resulting turbulent water is now much enjoyed by paddlers for slalom training.

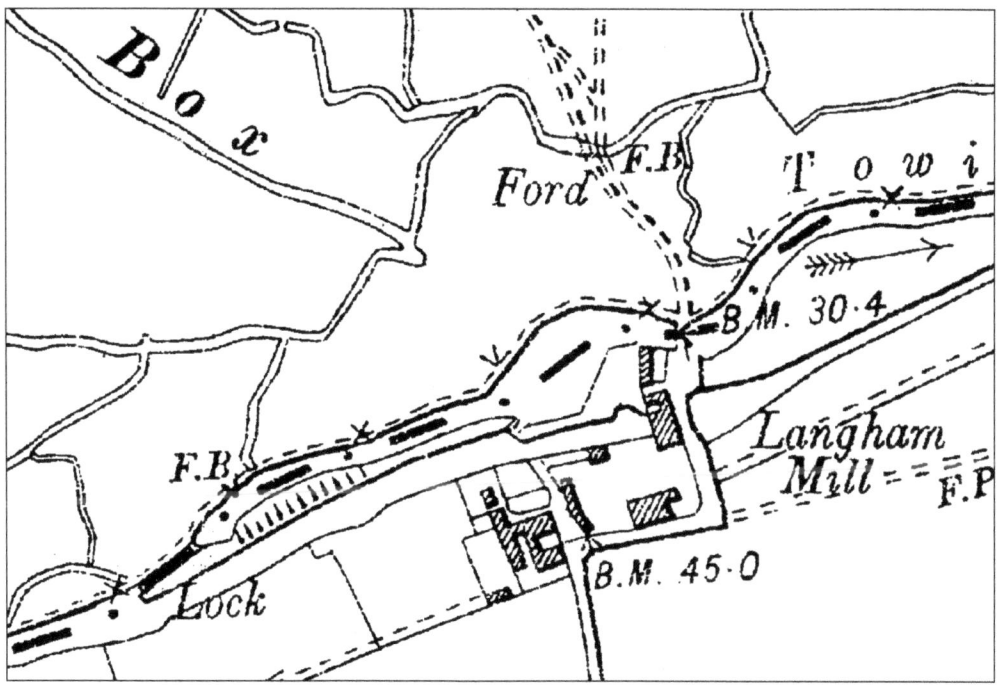

Rather unusually Langham Mill was astride a long mill race, with the original bypass channel made suitable for barge traffic in 1705. The present water pumping station, in addition to occupying the mill site, has expanded onto adjoining land. The lane leading to the river remains unchanged.

The lane to the river provides a convenient access for canoe trips. From here in 1955, the Inland Waterways Association held its first cruise to exercise the public right of navigation, receiving support from local paddlers and canoeists from Ipswich and Chelmsford. The party started just below the old cart-bridge, which enabled them to enter the water from the Suffolk bank. The bridge collapsed a few years later and has since been replaced by a modern footbridge.

Following the success of the 1955 canoe cruise, it became customary to hold annual rallies of boats along the river. This party of single and double kayaks, plus a Canadian canoe, was captured on film in 1965, just downstream from Langham.

Four
Stratford St Mary to Dedham

A Victorian lady stands besides the upper pair of gates at Stratford St Mary Lock, c.1900. There is substantial leakage, and vegetation is growing from the lock wall, an indication that the Navigation Company was spending little money on maintenance. In the 1930s the lock was completely rebuilt and replaced by the present concrete-sided structure.

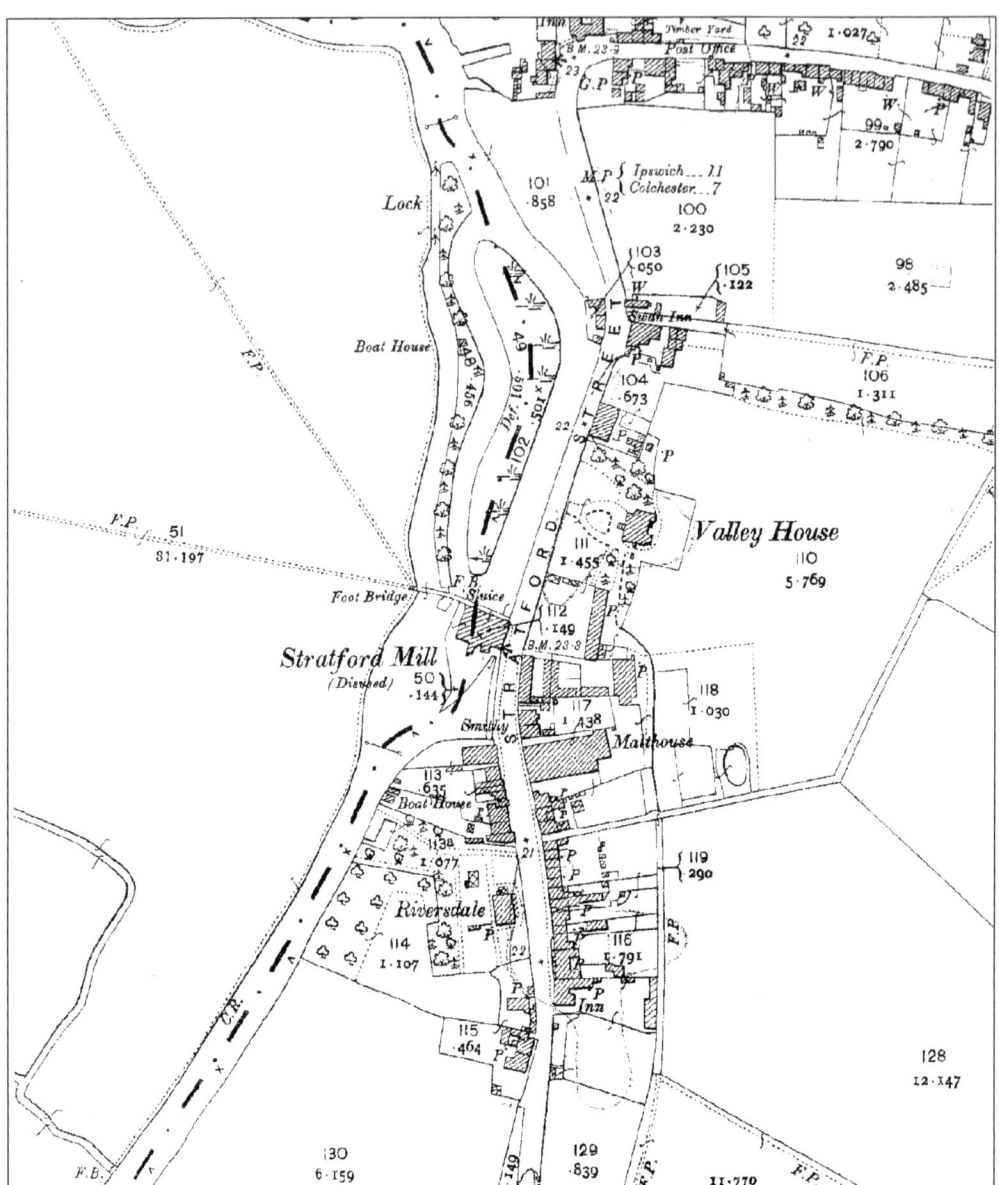

Most locks on the Stour were built immediately next to the mill. However, at Stratford St Mary a separate navigation channel, some 700ft long, exists parallel to the mill-race. It was probably built in the nineteenth century when an attempt was made to improve navigation to compete for trade against the newly built railways. The 1705 lock was probably on the site of the present bypass weir. Today, the cut is badly silted, but both it and the lock are subject to restoration proposals.

Stratford St Mary Lock, c.1900. In Victorian times, and until the late 1950s, a boat hire station existed in the lock cut.

Since the formation of the River Stour Trust in 1968 regular working parties have been held to clear the lock of trees and undergrowth, pending full restoration. This picture was taken after one of the first working parties in 1970. The Trust now intends to restore the lock fully in 2002. This will involve dredging out the Cut, removing silt from the chamber, installing new gates and erecting facsimile crossbeams.

Mr Norfolk, who lived nearby, was for many years the owner of the rowing boat station at Stratford St Mary. He is pictured here in 1955, over ninety years old, standing on his landing stage. His boats were stationed on both the upper and lower reaches of the river and were portaged from one channel to the other by means of a stout winch, which although long disused, remains in position today. Mr Norfolk died in the late 1950s.

Mr Norfolk's moorings in Stratford St Mary Lock Cut, 1955.

The exit to Stratford St Mary Lock Cut from the millpond, c.1900. A footbridge provided by the Navigation Company gave access to a path from the village to Langham. On the right is a glimpse of the already derelict Stratford St Mary Mill. It was demolished some years later and the site eventually acquired by the Water Company.

The eighteenth century landscape paintings of John Constable have made the river famous for its barge traffic; nevertheless, it has always been used for pleasure as well. In Victorian times there were many hire boat stations and some of the mill proprietors had their own steam launches. Today, the river is used for recreational purposes only. This handsome traditional punt, owned by the Jeffries family, was captured on film at Stratford St Mary in 1993.

At the turn of the nineteenth century there was a busy lime kiln at Stratford St Mary Bridge, receiving cargoes of chalk from Ballingdon. After firing, the lime was carted to Colchester for use in the building industry, or spread on nearby fields. The moored barge has a load of timber and there is a stack of bricks on the quay.

After the closure of the kiln the proprietor's house was extended and converted into a high-class restaurant, known as La Talbooth, seen here c.1935. Today it remains a venue for gastronomic enthusiasts and has an international reputation.

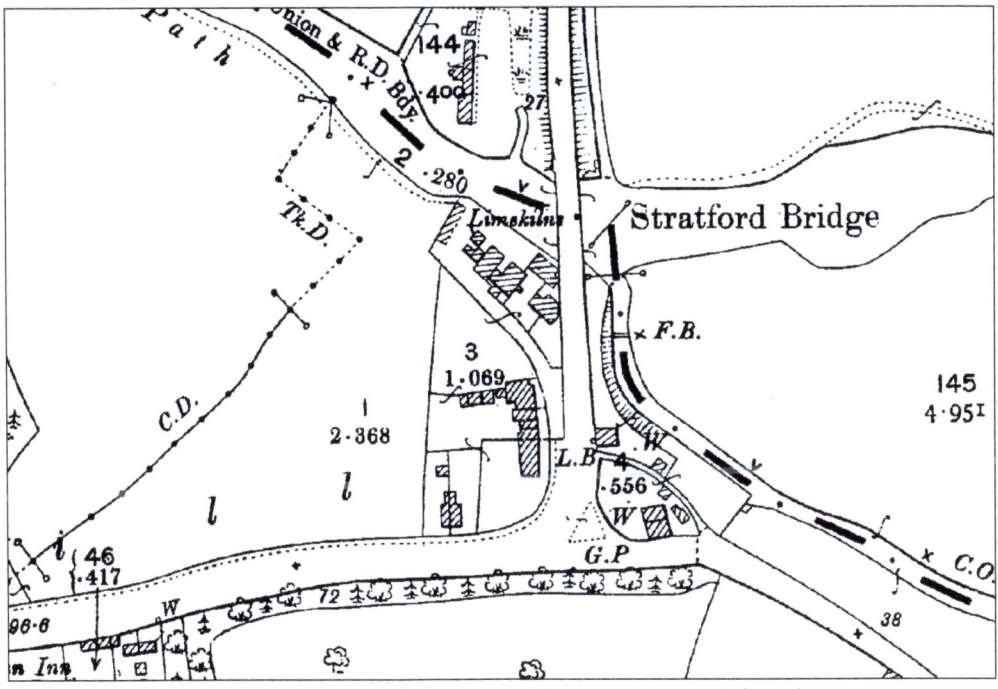

This map, c.1900, illustrates the superb location of the lime kilns and the subsequent restaurant in relation to the main road from Colchester to Ipswich. A coal wharf serving the village also existed nearby. During the late 1950s the old road was bypassed and a trunk road now cuts through the water meadows to the right.

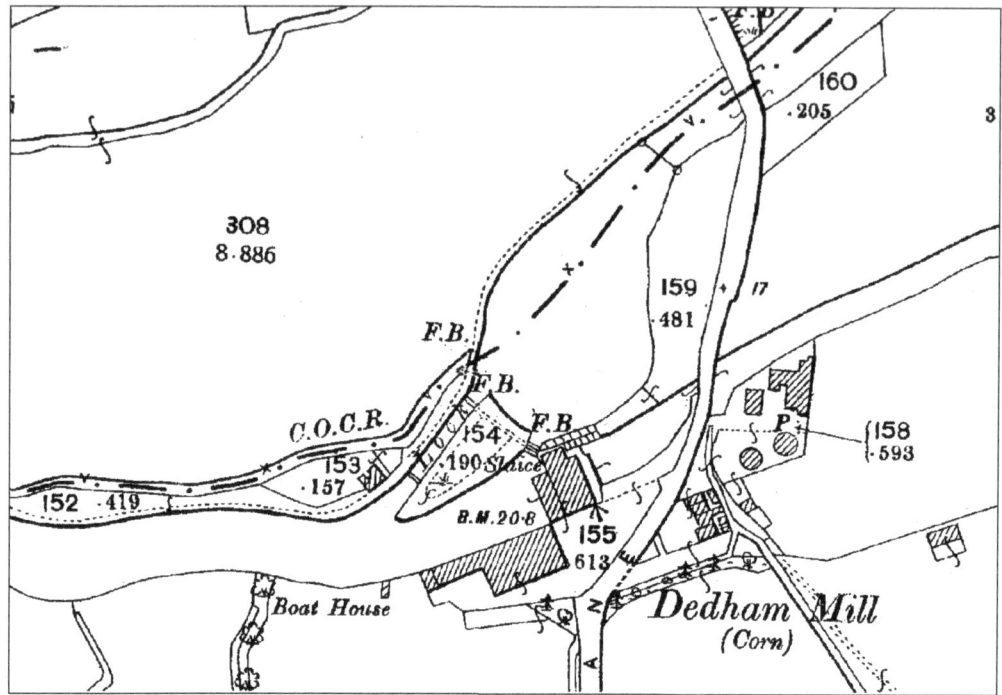

Throughout the nineteenth century, Dedham made extensive use of the river with coal and wheat delivered to the mill. Coal was also unloaded at the town's small gas works downstream. Flour was a return cargo to Mistley. Even in those days, tourism was an important industry, with a substantial boathouse and cafe next to the bridge. Boats were also available for hire at the lock house.

The downstream gates and crossbeams of Dedham lock were accurately shown in this detailed black and white sketch, c.1900. The substantial staging, on which the boy is laying, is part of a wooden causeway extension to the towpath.

Five

Dedham to Flatford

Dedham Lock, c.1900, when it was still of timber construction, with a moored lighter upstream. The broad well-trampled towpath used by the barge horses passes in front of the lock house hedge.

Dedham Lock and barge, c.1900, provide a picturesque setting for this family group. The eye of the artist with sketch board and pallet may have been attracted to the unusual gothic style lock house just out of view.

Happily posing for the photographer, c.1900, the Lock keeper steadies his rowing boat. Its high sides indicate it was built for estuary work and may have come second hand from Mistley. A chair has been brought from the house for his wife, who obviously didn't think the occasion important enough to remove her apron!

Dedham, like the locks at Stratford, Flatford and Brantham, was rebuilt at the expense of the Waterworks Company in the early 1930s, but became unusable due to lack of maintenance. In 1955, members of the Inland Waterways Association attempted to pass boats through but, despite their best efforts, were unable to close jammed upper gates. As at Stratford, the replacement chamber was built entirely of mass concrete, but the gates were similar to the originals.

Another picture of the same expedition by the Inland Waterways Association with the participants clustered around the lower gates. The picture was taken from almost the same spot as that on pages 86 and 87. The author stands on the far left.

In 1990 the Environment Agency decided to make use of Dedham Lock for flood control purposes by inserting a tilting weir into the floor of the lock. This picture was taken whilst construction work was in progress.

Concurrently with the work of the Environment Agency, the River Stour Trust removed, reboarded and replaced the existing gates, thus reopening the lock for navigational use. Colin Langstone, a professional lock gate maker from Hatfield Peverel, watches his assistant working.

One of the first boats to pass through Dedham Lock in 1990 was the River Stour Trust's own boat '*Stour Trusty*' Those on board include, on the right, Doug Barrett and next to him is the Trust chairman, Tony Platt.

Since restoration, Dedham Lock is regularly used by pleasure craft. This shot was taken during a recent rally of boats from Sudbury to Brantham, when a variety of light craft crammed into the chamber, pleased to avoid a difficult portage.

A close-up of the lower pair of gates. To comply with present day Health and Safety regulations a handrail has been installed alongside the platform. A major contributor to the restoration was the Essex Heritage Trust whose help is commemorated by a plaque fitted to the gates.

Another view of the restored lower gates. The gates and their unique paddle gear are replicas of those used on the original lock. The paddle is raised or lowered by winding the attached chain around the small horizontal capstan.

Although probably originally a coal wharf, for at least 100 years the Boathouse next to the bridge at Dedham, seen here c.1910, has been a popular amenity for local residents and visitors. During the mid 1900s the proprietor specialised in building small yachts, which he delivered via the waterway to estuary customers. Recently, the boathouse has been attractively renovated and remains as well visited as ever.

A fascinating aerial picture of Flatford, c.1995. The original lock, the subject of many of John Constable's landscape scenes, was sited immediately on the right of the existing structure but was infilled when the navigation was improved in the nineteenth century.

Six
Flatford to Brantham and Mistley

John Constable, the eighteenth-century landscape artist, lived for a time at Flatford Mill. Many of his canvases showed the river in its heyday as a busy commercial waterway with its unique lighters carrying their loads along the navigation.

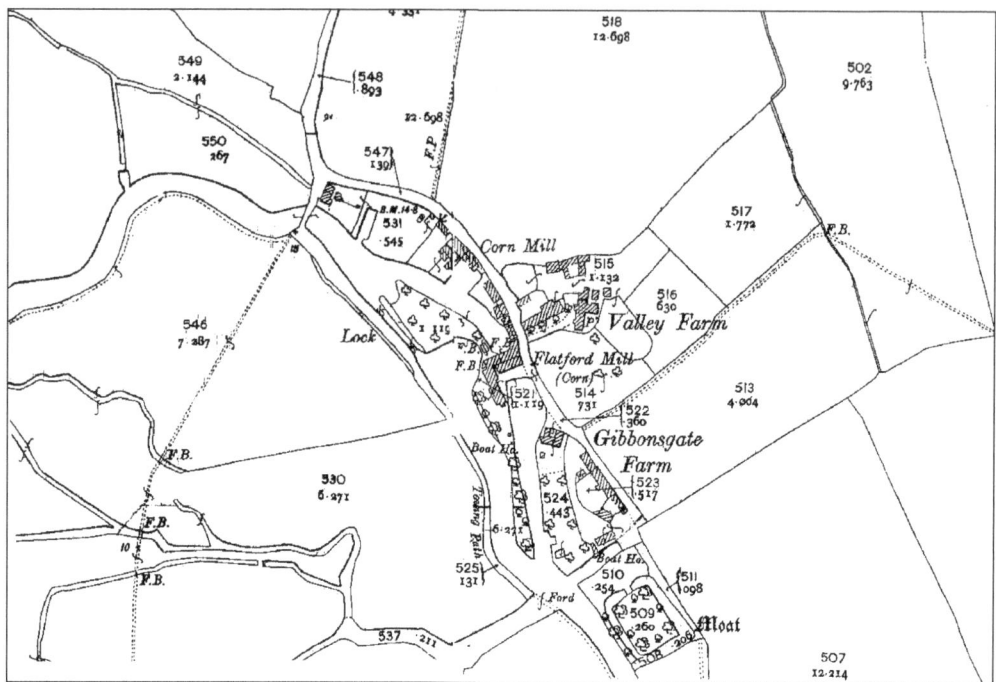

The various navigation features at Flatford are clearly identified on this map, c.1890. The original turf sided lock, as painted by John Constable, was sited next to the existing lock. Upstream is the barge building and repair dock, whilst on the same side and nearer the mill there is a further basin which once provided water access to a granary. In recent years the granary has become a museum and the basin has been infilled. In the 1980s the barge building dock was rediscovered and restored by the National Trust and the River Stour Trust and is now a popular visitor attraction.

This delightful, c.1900, boating scene shows two ladies about to pass under Flatford Bridge. Rowing boats could be hired at the Bridge Cottage.

From pre-war days Bridge Cottage, shown here c.1955, was a popular destination for those wanting a quiet day on the river. Tea and cakes were also available. In the 1980s the premises were acquired by the National Trust who established a John Constable and Dedham Vale Interpretation Centre, together with a smart restaurant alongside. Boat hire moved to a new location immediately upstream.

Flatford Lock, c.1900, was of timber construction, but by the 1920s it had fallen into a ruinous condition, and was only operable with difficulty. It was rebuilt in mass concrete by the Water Company, in return for the Navigation Company agreeing to the abstraction of water from the river.

A lighter emerging from Flatford Lock, c.1905, with the barge horse standing ready to take the strain. Although through traffic ceased on the navigation about the time of the First World War, a pair of boats operated between Dedham and Mistley until the late 1920s.

In a scene reminiscent of many of John Constable's paintings of Dedham Vale, a pair of lighters are proceeding upstream from Flatford Lock, c.1905. The remains of the original 1705 lock can just be spotted to the left of the chamber.

A pair of lighters drift slowly downstream towards Flatford Lock, c.1905. Bridge Cottage was then occupied by two families.

An official photograph of Flatford Lock, shortly after it was rebuilt in the early 1930s by the water company. Of particular interest is the diagrammatic cross section showing the construction of the lock walls. The photographer was Leslie Pollard, a young civil engineer who designed and supervised the construction work

In 1990 the Environment Agency instituted a flood control scheme on the lower part of the Stour including the installation of tilting gates midway along the chambers at Dedham and Flatford. Here, an engineer is carrying out a full survey prior to design work being undertaken. When not in use the tilting gate lies on the bed of the chamber.

After rebuilding in the 1930s, Flatford Lock slowly became unusable, due to lack of maintenance. In 1975, as one of their first projects, the River Stour Trust organised a series of voluntary working parties to restore the lock. This involved the removal of tons of mud and silt from the chamber and making the existing gates watertight by tarring and covering with resin bonded plywood.

On Easter Day 1975 the Lock was reopened for use. The first boat to enter the chamber was the *Lady Caroline*, skippered by Hugh Turner. The passengers included Lord Greenwood of Rossendale, then President of the Trust. As Tony Greenwood MP, he had previously been Minister of Housing and Local Government in the post war Labour Government.

Lord Greenwood cuts the tape from the fore deck of the *Lady Caroline*, declaring Flatford Lock open to the public. Immediately behind him stands Trust member Wilf Peake and to the left, with capstan bar, Frank Frecknall.

Lord Greenwood was an enthusiastic supporter of the Trust. His message published in a special souvenir issue of its journal is reproduced here.

The River Stour Trust is to me one of the most exciting organisations with which I am associated and I have boundless admiration for those of its members who give their time and energy so generously to protect, restore, and enhance one of our most beautiful rivers.

The Stour is a very English river, gentle and welcoming, and its scale is just right; it is no coincidence that it inspired two of our greatest painters.

To me, as to thousands of others, the river gives endless pleasure (increasingly so as the work of the Trust progresses), and all of us owe an immense debt to those whose own sacrifices yield such a high dividend for the rest of us.

Greenwood of Rossendale

Although the lock was successfully re-opened, by 1990 the lock gates were again in poor condition; they leaked badly and needed replacement. A national appeal was launched and RTZ, the international mining company, offered to sponsor the work. In December 1991 completely new oak gates, built at Hatfield Peverel, Essex, were installed by Colin Langstone.

The Lock was officially re-opened in May 1992 by John Constable, current President of the River Stour Trust and a descendant of the eighteenth century landscape artist. The first boat through the lock was the Trust's own motor boat, *Stour Trusty*, since replaced by an Edwardian style electric launch. She was accompanied by various rowing boats, canoes and a punt.

Flatford Lock in 1992, soon after the installation of the new gates. Other work carried out at the same time was the installation of new crossbeams, or lintels, to maintain the traditional appearance, and the replacement of formwork covering the concrete at the lock entrance and exit.

On hearing of the acquisition of Bridge Cottage by the National Trust in 1984, members of the River Stour Trust immediately offered to clear the debris infilling the old barge building dry dock which lay within the boundary of the property. This picture shows the site before clearance started.

Trust members hoped that under the debris the remains of a barge might be found. According to tradition it was left on the stocks when the skipper died. The remains of a barge with its back broken in several places and the bow missing were indeed found. Attempts were made to remove it but, sadly, it disintegrated.

After the remains of the dry dock were excavated, the National Trust carried out an accurate reconstruction, using unpublished sketches by John Constable as a guide. The River Stour Trust hope eventually to build a replica barge in the dock using traditional boat building skills.

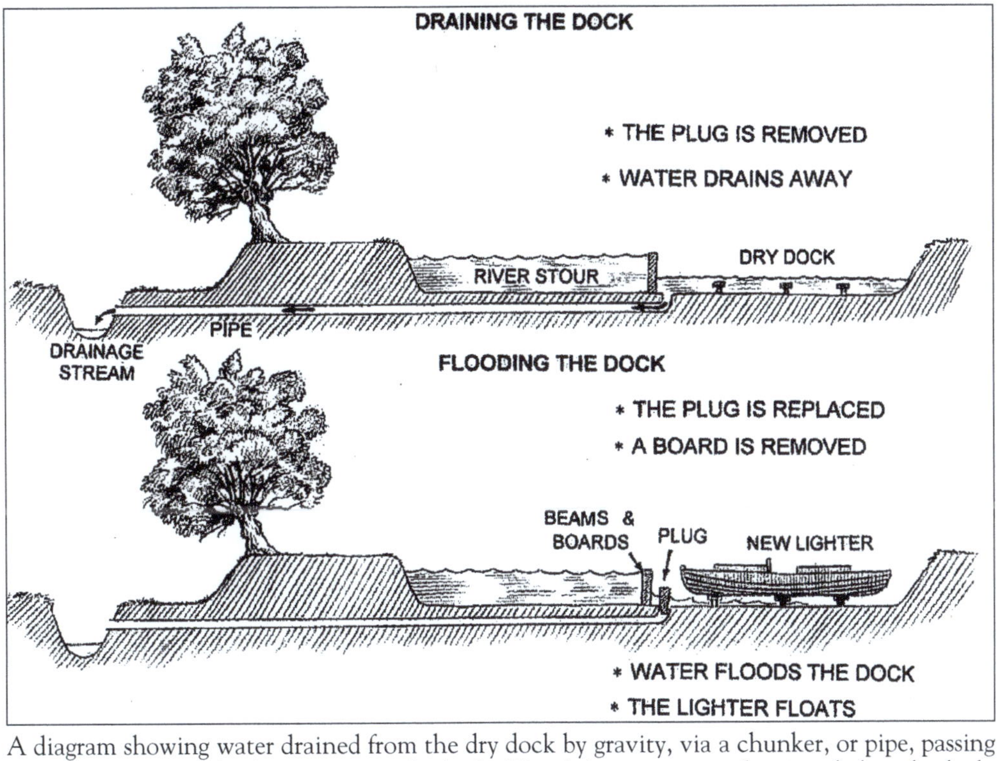

A diagram showing water drained from the dry dock by gravity, via a chunker, or pipe, passing under the river, to discharge into a side ditch. This fed in turn into the river below the lock. Entry to the dock was gained through a simple flash weir, consisting of removable cross beams and watertight boards.

A pair of lighters being towed downstream below Flatford, c.1900, with a youth riding the barge horse. The tall chimney in the distance is that of Flatford Steam Mill, demolished in 1929.

Due to the caprices of the various landowners the towpath frequently changed sides. Consequently, horses were trained to jump onto especially strengthened fore decks, the barge then being punted to the far side of the river. This photo dates from c.1900.

Whilst the barge was crossing, the horse was trained to remain very still until required to jump onto the opposite bank. Although passengers were not normally permitted, on this occasion, c.1900, a young boy has been able to cadge a lift.

Taken c.1900, this picture demonstrates the size and strength of the wooden barges. The horse is preparing to jump onto the towpath.

Whenever possible bargemen supplemented their rather Spartan diet. Many set eel traps at likely spots and inspected them as they floated passed. This bargeman, c.1900, has just cleared several for his supper, most likely cooking them on his cabin stove.

In almost idyllic surroundings, a pair of lighters proceed towards Flatford. A continuous row of pollarded willows marked the line of the towpath.

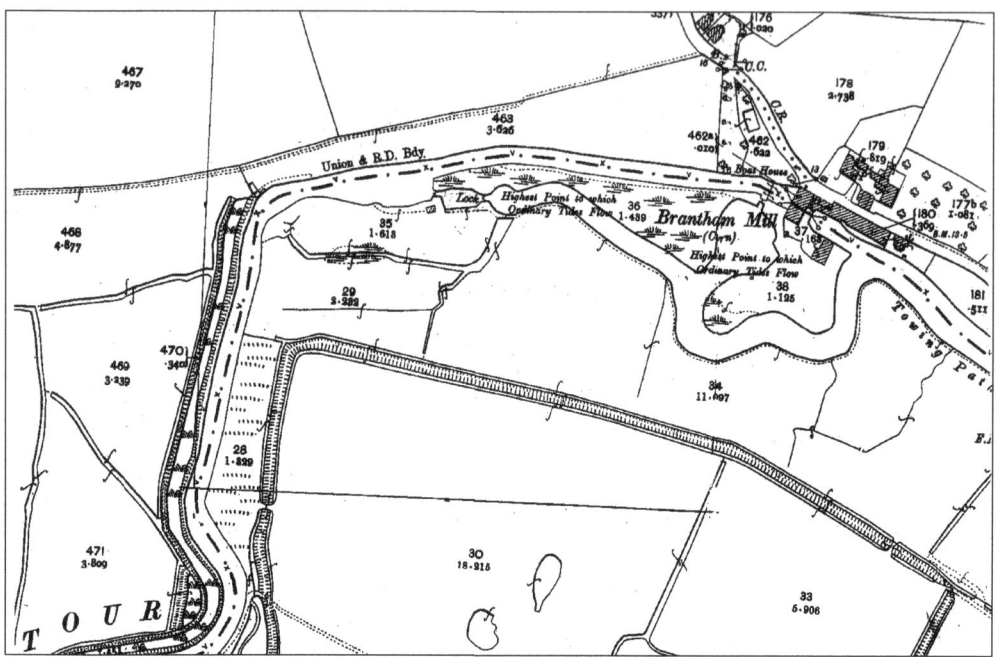

In 1971, the Brantham Barrage, about half a mile downstream from the lock, was built to prevent salt water from penetrating upstream towards Flatford. Until then, the river became tidal at the lock and mill site. This map, c.1900, shows Brantham Mill, on the tidal limit, when it was still a functioning corn mill. It was demolished in the 1960s, although it ceased to be used for milling many years earlier.

Brantham Lock differed from all the other locks on the river, being wide enough to hold six lighters, as only at high tide was there sufficient depth of water to float boats to and from Mistley. Like the three upstream locks, it was rebuilt by the water company in the 1930s. It is pictured here in 1955, with the tide on the ebb.

Brantham Lock, c.1900, with a pair of lighters entering at high water from the tidal estuary.

When in 1955 the Inland Waterways Association first started to hold annual cruises of boats along the river, it was still possible, with difficulty, to operate Brantham Lock. Here, six canoes wait in the chamber for the lower gates to be opened. Brantham Mill is seen in the distance. As a result of the construction of Brantham Barrage there is now no change of level and the gates have been removed.

Canoeists making the annual cruise down the River Stour, on Sunday, to maintain the public right of navigation, and pictured near Brantham. Below, left to right, Mr J. E. Marriage, chairman River Stour Action Committee, organisers of the cruise, Mrs Joan Goff, secretary, and Mr W. Peeke, commodore Stour Sailing Club.

The Inland Waterways Association continued to hold their annual cruise along the river until 1968, when the River Stour Trust took over its local activities. On 29th September 1967 this report appeared in the local newspaper.

Whilst Parliamentary approval was being sought for the construction of Brantham Barrage, the IWA and the Trust jointly requested that a lock should be included to allow continued boat access to and from the estuary. The authorities would not agree to this but instead built a boat roller ramp. Sadly, it is evident that when photographed in 1998, maintenance work by the navigation authority left much to be desired.

The area above the barrage has become a popular venue for canoe and dinghy events due to its proximity to the boat roller ramp and several boat jetties. This was the scene in September 1974, when a rally was held to raise funds for the Royal National Lifeboat Institute.

The transhipment point for goods barged up and down the river was Mistley, then a small busy port. Two or three gangs of Stour lighters would be breasted together and quanted, or poled, up or down the tideway. Sometimes, when there was a favourable wind, a crude sail would be

rigged up. In this picture, c.1900, the crews of two pairs quant their vessels downstream, as two passengers enjoy the trip.

The terminus for the lighters was the quay at Mistley, where cargoes were transferred directly to and from the sailing vessels. Here, c.1900, several lighters are moored alongside a brig. One boat has the hatch covers removed, enabling stevedoring to take place. The presence of railway wagons on the quay indicates competition between water and rail use.

Another view of the same Mistley quay, *c.*1900, with several lighters moored alongside a Thames sailing barge. Sailing barges were extensively used along the East Coast and Thames Estuary. Their great asset was a very shallow draft, enabling them to penetrate the tiny wharves serving farms and villages at the head of the tideway.

This view of Mistley quay from upstream, *c.*1900, shows a number of Stour lighters moored alongside two Thames sailing Barges. In the distance is one of the massive waterside mills, which existed until the 1960s.

Many of the barges which traded along the Stour were sunk about 1916 in Ballingdon Cut and the horses shot, apparently to prevent the German army from making use of them should they invade. As a result of the development of motor transport the boats were not raised after the War, but gradually filled with silt and became overgrown by rushes and other aquatic plants. In 1973, members of the River Stour Trust, assisted by the Sudbury Historical Society, excavated a barge from the mud. Surprisingly, although the upper part of the boat had disintegrated due to exposure to the air, the lower part remained in reasonable condition and, once the mud was removed, floated with few problems. In a considerable act of faith, the boat was towed down stream to a temporary berth at Great Cornard. As a gesture of thanks, all the people who had assisted in its recovery were invited to make the trip.

Seven
Restoring a Lighter

In the early 1960s the water level in Ballingdon Cut was permanently lowered as part of a flood prevention scheme. This caused the upper parts of the lighters, sunk in 1916, to be exposed and rapid decay set in. The remains can be seen clearly although covered with dense plant growth.

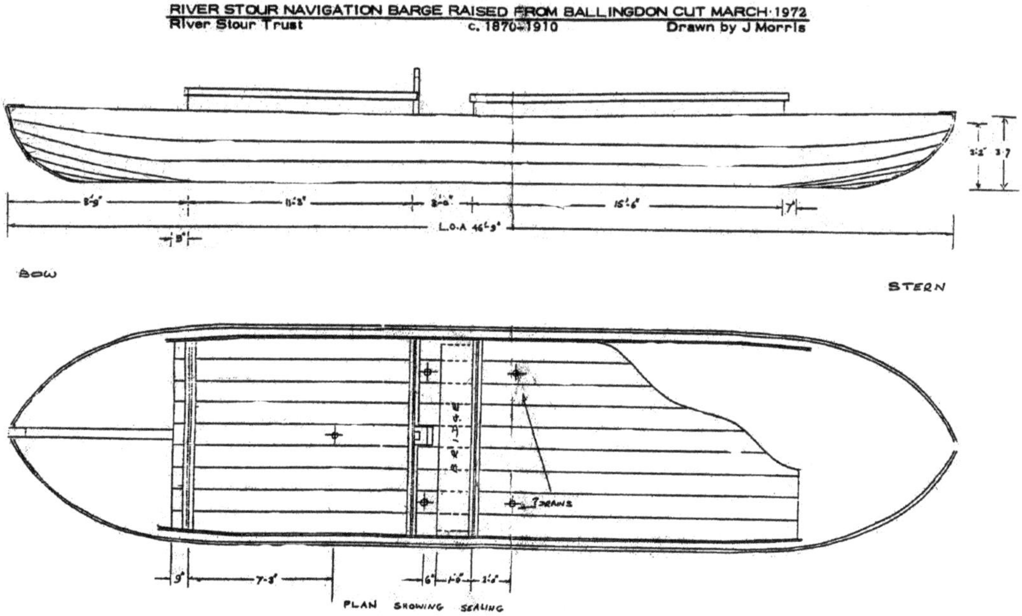

Before any works of restoration could be started on the recovered hulk, an accurate survey of the boat was carried out and working drawings prepared. Plans subsequently used to guide restoration were based on some of the photographs reproduced in this present book, and also sketches drawn by John Constable. The prepared plans shown here are probably the first ever as the original builders would have carried all the details in their head.

Following removal to Great Cornard, the remains of the lighter were floated into a specially prepared dry dock near the Mill. Here the timbers were coated with special preservative and some preliminary repairs undertaken.

In 1977 the Trust commenced the restoration of the Stour Lighter, through a government sponsored Job Creation Scheme, whereby the Trust employed, at government expense, five unemployed men. The Trust was responsible for the provision of tools and materials. The boat was moved to a property in Middleton Road, where over an eighteen-month period the work was carried out. Roy Porter, the foreman, is shown here. Technical instruction was provided by Frank Frecknall, a Trust member.

Much of the barge had to be rebuilt, particularly at the bow and stern, where the original timber had rotted away. Steam heating was used to give the necessary curved shape to the replacement oak planks.

The deck and hatches were completely rebuilt and new floor boards installed. Here, the replacement hatch covers are being constructed and placed in position over the two holds.

Towards the completion of the restoration, the Trust held an open day in which the public was invited to view the boat. Among those visiting was an old bargeman, pictured here on the ladder talking to Roy Porter.

With assistance from the 819th Civil Engineering Squadron, United States Air force, based at Wethersfield, the boat was returned to a temporary wet berth at Great Cornard in March 1980.

Throughout the 1980s the lighter made a number of promotional trips along the river at Sudbury. She was towed in the traditional manner by *Snowy*, owned by Francis Batten, then Chairman of the Trust. The two crew members were Frank Frecknall (left) and Jack Leveridge (right).

The River Stour Trust

The River Stour Trust was formed in 1968 as a campaigning body to conserve and maintain the right of navigation on the river and is committed to the restoration of through navigation between Sudbury and the estuary. They recognise this must be undertaken in tandem with the preservation and enhancement of the natural environment, in particular the beauty and tranquillity of the Stour Valley. To this end, they encourage responsibility and harmonious enjoyment of the river by all users.

One of the Trust's early successes was to achieve, on appeal to the House of Lords, an amendment to the Anglian Water Authority Act to ensure that the river continued as a statutory navigation and to be available to boat users.

Since its formation, the Trust has restored lengths of the river to through navigation, including the locks at Flatford and Dedham, made famous by the paintings of John Constable. In September 1997, a completely new lock was opened at Great Cornard. This project received half of its funding from the National Lottery via the Millennium Commission. Preparatory work has now begun on the restoration of Stratford Lock. The Trust has also restored one of the original lighters, which used to carry goods to and from Mistley and Sudbury. It is berthed at Great Cornard, adjacent to the new lock. It is the only remaining vessel of its type.

The Trust has restored both the former Navigation Company's Quay Basin area of Sudbury and a derelict eighteenth century Grade II listed building – The Granary at Quay Lane. The latter is now its headquarters and incorporates an Interpretative Centre and a small museum; as well as offering a meetings/functions room for weddings, social and business events.

The Trust is acutely conscious of the need to preserve and enhance the natural environment in conjunction with its restoration plans for the river structures. Restoration of the Quay Basin has recreated many habitats and encouraged a variety of flora and fauna within the water and its surroundings. The new lock at Great Cornard has enabled the planting of 185 trees (native species) and the creation of an adjacent wildlife haven.

The Trust offers trips aboard its environmentally friendly, silent, electric launches: – *Stour Trusty II* at Flatford, and *Rosette* at Sudbury. It also facilitates canoeing and boating activities, as well as organising a regular programme each year. This includes water-based activities (the Lengths man's Cruise, Boat Rally, canoeing meets, family picnics, etc.) and land based activities, including events such as Steam days, and Open Days at The Granary, with its tea-room and museum. The Trust's journal, *Lock Lintel*, is issued free of charge to all members three times a year.

Membership of the River Stour Trust:

Anyone with an interest in conservation, navigation and preservation of the local heritage is invited to join the Trust. Please write to:

The Membership Secretary
River Stour Trust
The Granary
Quay Lane
Sudbury
Suffolk   Telephone: 01787 313199
CO10 2AN   Website: www.riverstourtrust.org

Further Information:

Although the whole of the river between Sudbury and the estuary can be used by manually propelled craft, current Environment Agency bylaws restrict powered craft (with a few exceptions) to the reaches between Sudbury and Great Henny. Further details can be obtained from the Environment Agency, Kingfisher House, Orton Way, Peterborough PE2 5ZR.

All three operative locks are under the control of the River Stour Trust, with whom prior arrangements for their use should be made.

The towpath was never a right of way and only isolated sections are available for public use.

Acknowledgements

The photographs and illustrations appear by kind permission of the following: Leigh Alston, Robert Baker, Paul Beverstock, Eric Boesch, Robert Cook, G.R. Mortimer, Ted Pearson, River Stour Trust, Sudbury Rowing Club, Vestry House Museum and Michael Woodward. Others are from the author's own collection. I also acknowledge the help given by my wife, Marion, who cheerfully corrected the grammatical and spelling errors, and made many invaluable suggestions as to the content.